RAISING CAIN,

FLEEING EGYPT,

AND

FIGHTING PHILISTINES

Smyth & Helwys Publishing, Inc.
6316 Peake Road
Macon, Georgia 31210-3960
1-800-747-3016
©2006 by Smyth & Helwys Publishing

Library of Congress Cataloging-in-Publication Data

McEntire, Mark Harold, 1960-
Raising Cain, fleeing Egypt, and fighting Philistines : the Old Testament in popular music /
by Mark McEntire and Joel Emerson.
p. cm.
Includes bibliographical references and index.
ISBN 978-1-57312-464-5
1. Bible. O.T.—Criticism, interpretation, etc.
2. Bible in music.
3. Popular music—Religious aspects—Christianity.
4. Bible. O.T.—Influence.
I. Emerson, Joel.
II. Title.
BS1171.3.M44 2006
221.6—dc22

2005037666

Raising Cain, Fleeing Egypt,
and Fighting Philistines:
The Old Testament in Popular Music

By Mark McEntire and Joel Emerson

Contents

Introduction

On his 1978 album *Darkness on the Edge of Town,* between the determined, poetic intensity of a song called "Badlands" and a haunting ballad called "Something in the Night," Bruce Springsteen's distinctive voice thunders:

In the Bible Cain slew Abel,
and east of Eden he was cast.
You're born into this life paying
for the sins of somebody else's past.
Daddy worked his whole life
for nothing but the pain.
Now he walks these empty rooms,
looking for someone to blame.
You inherit the sins,
you inherit the flames.
Adam raised a Cain . . . .

In the midst of an effort to produce an artistic expression of the pain and disappointment that often characterize human existence, Springsteen needed an image that was up to the task. He found one from the fourth chapter of Genesis. He was certainly not the first artist to find a necessary resource in the stories of the Bible's first family. Seventeen years later, with the release of his critically acclaimed compact disc *The Ghost of Tom Joad*, Springsteen and the world seemed prepared for the full realization that he had become rock-and-roll's Steinbeck, and while he derived the title of the record from *The Grapes of Wrath*, the songs resonate just as fully with *East of Eden*. He is one of many popular songwriters and performers fed by the biblical tradition, among other resources.

What separates "high culture" from "popular culture"? It is difficult to imagine an answer to this question that would not seem biased and elitist. The line between the two must be blurry. We expect a number of things from good art. We expect it to grab us emotionally and to make us think. We expect it to reveal the truth, whether in great beauty or ugliness. We expect it to bring us either pleasure or pain, or both. We expect art to help us make sense of life, to connect its disjointed aspects, to provide us with "aha!" moments. It is because of these great expectations that no consensus can be reached on what constitutes good art. The lyrics of popular music do not always rise to the level of great poetry, but it would be a mistake to think great poetry does not reside in this aspect of modern culture. Popular music operates at a variety of levels, from the depth and complexity of songwriters like Springsteen, Bob Dylan, and Natalie Merchant to the shallow, nonsense lyrics of many songs that populate the Top 40 list.

One of the factors that sometimes provides art with a richer sense of texture is its ability to draw an allusion to the classic expressions of human culture, thought, and experience. As a student of the Old Testament, I am as interested in the reception of the biblical text as I am in its production and transmission. One of the ways the biblical text is received is through its incorporation into works of art, whether they be the plays of Shakespeare, the paintings of Rembrandt, the novels of Flannery O'Connor, the films of Martin Scorsese, or the sculptures of Michelangelo. I became interested some years ago in the use of the Bible in popular music and began to notice when quotations, names, and images from the Bible were incorporated into musical lyrics, so I started developing a list of such songs. I began assigning students in my classes to write an essay about a popular song that makes use of a specific biblical text.[1] This has allowed me to enlarge my list of songs that use Old Testament references, so that it now tops 100.

When I decided to try to develop a resource dealing specifically with the subject of Old Testament references in popular music, I first thought of simply producing a catalogue of examples along with brief discussions and evaluations. As I looked at the examples I had compiled, however, it struck me that they were not evenly distributed. Certain parts of the Old Testament seem to have captured the attention and imagination of modern songwriters more than others. Therefore, these uses of the Bible in song lyrics are clustered around certain sets of texts. This observation led to the idea of looking at these songs as clusters. Along with a discussion of the ways songwriters make use of biblical references, I hope also to raise questions about why they have found these particular areas of the Bible to be such a fertile resource for their artistic expression.

Numerous songs refer to texts in the early part of Genesis. Allusions to the creation and flood narratives are particularly common. Songs referring to texts in this part of the Bible will be discussed in chapter 1, "The First Family," and chapter 2, "Surviving the Storm." There are also a large number of songs that refer to texts within the patriarchal narratives. Songs in this group will be treated in chapter 3, "Family Matters." Chapter 4, "Let Me Out," will explore the cluster of songs that refer to aspects of the exodus story. It is surely no surprise that references to the legal material in popular music are difficult to find. The next identifiable cluster of songs are those that make use of heroic and villainous figures in the books of Joshua through Kings, such as Joshua, Samson, David, and Jezebel. These will be the subject of chapter 5, "The High and Mighty." The Old Testament contains its own musical lyrics within the poetry that fills many of its pages. The poetic material found in Psalms, Wisdom Literature, and Song of Songs also inspires modern poets. References to such texts will be in chapter 6, "The Poet's Poets."[2] Finally, modern songwriters sometimes place references to the prophetic literature in their songs. These will be examined in chapter 7, "Shouting in the Wind."

The selection of songs for this book has not been systematic. I cannot imagine a systematic way to do it. Readers will no doubt think of their own examples that have not been included. One of the purposes of the book, and one of the related assignments I give to students in my classes, is to raise the level of awareness of biblical references in popular music, so I hope readers will continue to add to the list. I am sure that early on, my list reflected my own preferences in musical styles or genres. As I have filled out the list with songs my students have directed to my attention, it has become more diverse. Rock and roll, country, hip-hop, folk, reggae, and selections from musical stage plays and movies are all included. Of course, these are overlapping styles of music that are classified as much for marketing purposes as for any other reason.[3]

The songs discussed in this book are ones that have relatively certain references to the Old Testament. It would be possible to move into an entirely different realm based upon varying definitions of "intertextuality." This would allow a discussion of songs that share a common pool of ideas with certain biblical texts but do not necessarily make any recognizable reference to them. In this case, the songwriter need not be aware of the connections. Michael J. Gilmour has moved in this direction in his excellent work on Bob Dylan and the Bible.[4] The nature of *Raising Cain* seemed to require a more definite sense of connection between song and biblical text. Of course, the use of a phrase or the name of a character from the Bible by no means indicates that the songwriter is fully aware of its location in the biblical text or of the biblical tradition surrounding it. Some phrases, such as "forbidden fruit," the "handwriting on the wall," or "an eye for an eye," have found their way into the American vernacular and are frequently used without awareness that they are derived from the Old Testament.

Interpreting literature is notoriously difficult and subjective. Meaning is an elusive prey. Without a direct statement from a songwriter, we cannot be sure what a song is supposed to be about or why a particular biblical reference has been incorporated into it. Recent trends in biblical interpretation have addressed the difficulty of determining the Bible's meaning by shifting the locus of meaning away from the author toward the interaction between text and reader.[5] We must acknowledge the role of the hearer in determining the meanings of songs as well. Interpretations of biblical texts and songs will be largely based on our own impressions. Thus, the discussions of biblical texts and songs that follow are intended to raise issues and invite dialogue rather than to provide definitive answers.

As a reader, teacher, and student of the Old Testament, I am generally pleased whenever it becomes the subject of conversation. I will attempt in every case to evaluate the effectiveness and appropriateness of particular references to the Old Testament without being proprietary. The Bible is the ultimate "public domain" source. It does not belong to anyone, and nobody can place restrictions on its use. Even if particular references to the Bible in songs may bother some people, sometimes one of the genuine purposes of art is to bother us. If a song causes me to think carefully or feel powerfully about something, including a biblical text, then it has played its role as art.

Readers will quickly notice that song lyrics are not provided in the text of this book. Copyright laws make such inclusion impossible. Where necessary in the discussion, brief segments of the lyrics are provided. Full use of this book will require acquisition of the lyrics of the songs. Consider using an Internet search engine, such as "Google." Simply type the title of the song in quotation marks, along with the word *lyrics*, not in quotation marks, and you will see a list of multiple sites.

One resource to consider is the ever-growing quantity of legal music sites for downloading songs. Services like iTunes.com, rhapsody.com, napster.com and the music services provided by Yahoo and MSN are just a few examples of easy-to-use download sites that will allow you to access many of the songs in this book on a song-by-song basis. Some will allow you to stream songs in their entirety for a low monthly fee while paying extra for the ability to make your own copy to a CD. Others will require you to purchase each track one at a time. All of them will allow you an easy, affordable way to have the songs to use both for your own personal work with the text as well as in small groups.

This book is aimed at a number of audiences. We hope it will be a valuable pedagogical resource in both the academy and the church. Devoted readers of the Bible may find new ways of thinking about this book through an examination of its connections to music. Those who enjoy listening to popular music may find their enjoyment enriched by a greater awareness of some its cultural roots.

Using the Study Questions

The discussion questions in the book are included in hopes of promoting small group discussion in many different environments. Churches, college and seminary classes, book clubs, or any group that finds itself engaged around the intersection of music and the great themes of the Old Testament should find these questions useful. Each numbered question has multiple questions within it, so if the group wanted, they could center an entire discussion on that broader set of questions rather than trying to tackle the entire chapter at once. Groups that meet for a sustained period could work through the entire chapter's questions if desired.

This provides great freedom in establishing your study as a short-subjects group that only meets for six or eight weeks, or you could set your structure for a longer period of time and still have plenty of questions to discuss. You might also encourage people to suggest other songs that approach a specific Old Testament text or theme in a certain way. Also, do not over-look the value of having your students explore their own creativity in writing poems and lyrics about the themes you examine. You might choose to make this an arts class where participants create using their specific skills and talents. In this scenario, you might use the book and discussion questions as a starting point.

Whatever your format, size, or context, remember that the songs emerge from the same human condition that the biblical text explores. Your group will have great success if you lean into the feelings and thoughts these great stories generate when they are read or heard anew, like in a song. It is in those times that the ink on the page seems to change color, and all of a sudden we relate to the people of the Old Testament in an entirely new way.

Notes

[1] This assignment must be defined precisely. Thousands of songs refer to one or more general religious ideas, such as love, hope, or faith. This assignment, however, requires a reference to a specific biblical text. I ask students to start by discussing that particular text. What is its context? What does it seem to mean? The second step is for them to analyze the song. What is the song about? What role does the biblical reference play in the song? The final step is to evaluate whether the use of the biblical reference in the song fits well with the meaning of the biblical text. It is possible for the biblical reference to be debatable. For example, while it is obvious that R.E.M.'s song "Man on the Moon" makes reference to Exodus 3, it is not as certain that Bob Dylan's "All Along the Watchtower" refers to Isaiah 21. Both of these songs will be discussed in more detail in later chapters. The former example illustrates another potential problem. While songs that mention certain biblical characters, such as Adam, Eve, Noah, or Samson, work as references to specific biblical texts of manageable size, the mere mention of the name of Moses or David is not enough. The lyric "Moses went walking with a staff of wood" is enough, however, to link the reference to Exodus 3.

[2] It has been common practice for a long time to take the words of Scripture, particularly from Psalms, and set them to music. Examples of this particular practice do not lend themselves to the kind of discussion in this book, nor to the classroom assignment mentioned above.

[3] There is a classification of music that is sometimes referred to as "Contemporary Christian Music." This classification is almost entirely a marketing scheme. Music marketed in this way falls within all of the genres listed above. Ultimately, this classification depends largely on the practices of record labels. Record stores need to categorize their merchandise. Generally, songs placed within this category display a surprising paucity of specific references to the Bible. Therefore, some examples will appear in the discussions that follow, but not a large number.

[4] See the discussion of intertextuality in Michael J. Gilmour, *Tangled Up in the Bible: Bob Dylan and Scripture* (New York: Continuum, 2004), 14-19.

[5] See the discussion of this trend in Mark Allan Powell, *What Is Narrative Criticism* (Minneapolis: Fortress Press, 1990), 1-10.

CHAPTER ONE

The First Family

Singing about Paradise and Pain

The Biblical Texts

The first three chapters of the Bible are an endless subject of fascination. They offer us two stunning stories of the origins of humanity and our surroundings. Genesis 1:1–2:4a[1] is remarkable in its majesty and rhythm. The seven-day account of God's creation of the universe has had a tremendous impact on the Western world. It forms the basis for the weekly cycle of our lives. It has been taken by many readers as a precise account of creation and has frequently been placed in opposition to modern, scientific conclusions about the origins of the universe and life. Others read it in a more metaphorical fashion and see in it a poetic expression of God's desire to bring order out of chaos. Nevertheless, this chapter presents tremendous problems as the opening passage of the biblical story. It offers no characters to follow and no clear setting for events to take place, so the question it raises is "Where can the story go from here?" It may be difficult to determine how the opening chapter of Genesis is related to the story of Adam and Eve in the Garden of

Eden found in Genesis 2:4b–3:24, but this second creation account solves the narrative problem raised by Genesis 1.[2]

Genesis 2–3 does not tell about the creation of humanity, but the forming and making of a man and a woman, Adam and Eve. It is not an account of the creation of "the heavens and the earth," but a story of the planting of a garden. Genesis 2:17 reports God's prohibition against eating from the "tree of knowledge, good and evil," and sets up the first potential conflict in the Bible, the stuff of which great stories are made. Genesis 2 reveals, when read carefully, that Eden is a geographical impossibility. The four rivers of 2:10-14 include the Tigris and Euphrates of Mesopotamia and the Gihon, or Blue Nile of Africa. These rivers likely represented the farthest points in opposite directions on the map of the world that was in the minds of Genesis's first audience. Eden is the place where these rivers all flow out of a single source. It is everywhere and nowhere at the same time. Eden is built for the imagination.

In this second story, the making of plants and animals is bracketed by the forming of a man and a woman. The strange story of God attempting to produce a suitable mate for the man leads to the making of the animals and ultimately to the "building" of the woman from a piece taken from the side of the man. The two humans are then united by marriage at the end of the chapter.

The wedded bliss with which Genesis 2 ends collapses in pain and alienation in Genesis 3. The story of the snake tempting Adam and Eve to eat the forbidden fruit, resulting in their expulsion from the Garden of Eden, is well known. The story has often been misunderstood in popular interpretation, however. Readers should be sure to notice that Adam is with Eve all along, that they are tempted together, eat together, and have their eyes opened together. This is the paradigmatic story of human limits, temptation, blame, and punishment for Western culture.[3] The intricate literary artistry of the story further magnifies these powerful themes. The characters are introduced at the beginning of the story in this order: Snake, Woman, Man. After the act of disobedience, God addresses the characters in the reverse order: Man, Woman, Snake. The order is reversed again, back to the original, when the punishments are handed out: Snake, Woman, Man. This literary feature serves to highlight all of the reversals taking place in the story. The punishments and their results include gender inequality, the pain and danger of childbirth, the resistance of the earth to fruitful labor, and, ultimately, death itself. When God casts the first two humans out of the Garden of Eden, God also provides clothing as protection for them. They move to the east, a direction Genesis consistently uses to represent movement away from the presence of God.[4] Yet, 4:1 reveals that God's presence is not entirely withdrawn.

The first story of human beings outside the Garden of Eden is also the story of the first murder. The murder of Abel by Cain in Genesis 4 is a painful and mystifying story. The two brothers are presented as opposites from the beginning, the farmer (Cain) and the shepherd (Abel). They come into conflict over the favor they are apparently shown, or not shown, by God. How do they know God has or has not "looked upon" their offerings? Perhaps Abel has simply been more successful than Cain. Is there some limit to God's blessings, though, that means only one of them can be blessed?[5] The theme of preference for the younger brother that pervades Genesis appears for the first time here, but the preference is not so one-sided. God speaks to Cain, the older brother, both before and after the murder. God does not speak to Abel, not even to warn him about Cain's jealousy and anger.

The book of Genesis favors the nomadic, shepherding way of life. Cain is, therefore, an "other" to the Israelites. Genesis 4:25 reports that Adam and Eve had a third son, Seth, to take the place of Abel, and Seth will continue Adam's genealogy, but prior to this a genealogy of Cain is provided in 4:17-22. This genealogy embodies the forces of progress and technology that proceed from Cain, the agriculturalist. Cain builds the first city, and his descendent, Tubal-Cain, is the first iron-worker. The more gentle Jabal (a shepherd) and Jubal (a musician) are included in Cain's genealogy, but they have names that resemble Abel's, just as their ways of life resemble his. Cain seems to have absorbed Abel's identity when he killed him. Cain's most prominent descendent, Lamech, magnifies Cain's violent tendencies and is remembered in the frightening little poem in 4:23-24.[6] The first family is divided, and these divisions grow as the genealogy that fills Genesis 5 moves the story quickly through ten generations from Adam to Noah.

Songs of Creation

Little wonder, considering the discussion above, that songwriters rarely make use of Genesis 1. It contains no conflict or romance or tragedy, the ingredients of human experience that make a good story. One notable exception to this observation is Spinal Tap's "Rock and Roll Creation." The lyrics of this song make significant use of phrases and images from Genesis 1. In an attempt to express the power and significance of the emergence of rock and roll music, this semi-mythical band found what it needed in the story of creation that emphasizes the emergence of light, order, and goodness from darkness, emptiness, and chaos. The voice of the singer, who is "feeling insignificant," finds meaning and purpose in this music, the kind of meaning and purpose that God is building into creation in Genesis 1. Thus, those things that come from God, such as "salvation" and "light," are interwoven in the third line of the song with the elements of music, such as "rhythm" and "sound." The creative potential of human beings thus mirrors the creation of God.

Unlike Genesis 1, Genesis 2–3 erupts into popular culture, with images of paradise, trees, apples, snakes, and sexuality. The power of its events and characters fuels works of art in varying mediums—novels, paintings, films, songs. Natalie Merchant's "Eden" plays lyrically with the tensions of human life. The incongruity of roses and thorns growing on the same bush expands into the mixture of joy and pain that characterizes human existence. The final stanza of the song proposes, perhaps in conflict with the biblical text, that paradise is still with us, even though it may be hidden. Instead of lying in the human past, this Eden lies in the future, an image of a better existence. This paradise requires a waking to its presence, though. The song illustrates our struggle with the concept of paradise and innocence. Is it something we all have and lose, and is it something we can regain? The final line of the song links Eden with heaven. This might seem to defy the contention in Genesis that Eden is a paradise to which we cannot return now that we have knowledge, but it is not an unprecedented move in either the Jewish or Christian tradition. Ezekiel takes the first step in coupling the vision of a rebuilt temple with images of the paradisal garden in Ezekiel 47. Revelation 22 finishes the transport of Eden into the future by using its images to portray a vision of heaven.

The bizarre story of the first man searching for a mate and naming all the animals in the process, from Genesis 2:18-20, is the centerpiece of Bob Dylan's "Man Gave Names to All the Animals." This song appeared on Dylan's *Slow Train Coming* album, which emerged from the period of his conversion to Christianity. While the chorus pulls in the opening line of the Bible, it is primarily about the story in Genesis 2. The playfulness of the song fills out a lack of detail in the biblical story of the naming of the animals, in which no animals are actually named. In the Bible, this story serves to introduce the creation of the man's counterpart, the first woman. Dylan does not mention the woman, however, and the twist at the end of the song moves in a different direction. This raises an issue that is not often mentioned in discussion of the text. Had the first man encountered the serpent before the serpent is introduced in Genesis 3?

Because Adam and Eve are the first named characters in the Bible, theirs becomes the paradigmatic romantic relationship. Genesis 2 ends with a wedding, and the notion of male and female being joined together is an irresistible image. Ani DiFranco is one of the most provocative songwriters of the past decade. The tension, pain, and disappointment of romantic relationships are the frequent subjects of her songs, so it is not surprising that she wrote one called "Adam and Eve." The words of the song are expressed in the first person voice of the woman, as the man with whom she had been involved the night before hurries away in the morning. The language is rough, angry, and explicit, but the anger of the first half of the song gives way to sorrow. The voice of the woman, who seems in the first verse to resist identification with Eve, acknowledges in the third verse that "I just happen to like apples and I am not afraid of snakes." The boldness of Eve and the reticence of Adam in the Genesis 3 story fuel the final verse in which the woman decides to move on and leave the man behind in the "ignorance" and "bliss" of his "garden."

Though the first line of Steven Tyler's "Adam's Apple" mentions Cain and Abel (Genesis 4), the song's primary referent is Genesis 3, as the title indicates. The first two verses play cleverly with the eating of forbidden fruit. Eve is both deceiver and deceived. The sexuality of this song is more subtle than in most of Aerosmith's music, but it is an undercurrent throughout the first two verses. In a surprisingly Augustinian reading of Genesis 3, Eve becomes "Adam's apple," and the sexual union of man and woman propels the song into the even more surprising third verse. The post-Eden world is the world of science to which human eyes are now opened, and an age-old question—"Was trading paradise for knowledge a good or bad bargain?"—hangs in the air as the song comes to an end.

The first reference to death in the Bible comes at the conclusion of the punishment sequence in Genesis 3:19. The familiar words are ". . . until your return unto the ground, for from it you were taken; for you are dust, and unto dust you shall return." These words in some form play a part in many funeral services and have become a familiar expression of the reality and finality of death. In "Bang the Drum Slowly," Emmylou Harris sings what she has identified as a eulogy for her father. The song extols both the simple hard work of its subject and his heroism, particularly in a time of war. The melody is a mesmerizing dirge that keeps returning to the central line of the chorus, "To dust be returning, from dust we begin." The pain of memory, loss, and regret throughout the song is offset by the reversal of this near quotation of Genesis 3:19. Life follows death, sorrow is muted by gratitude, and the singer realizes that her own life emerges from those that come before. This idea is expressed in the beautiful line, "But the songs of my life will still be sung, by the light of the moon you hung." The return to dust allows a new beginning, illuminated by the life that has gone before.

Songs East of Eden

The *cherubim* and the flaming, twisting sword God places on the east side of the Garden of Eden form the boundary between this section and the previous one, just as they form a boundary between the lost paradise and the place where life goes on. Bob Dylan's "Gates of Eden" speaks of this barrier, but it looks from the outside in, so it belongs on this side of the boundary. Like many of Dylan's early songs, "The Gates of Eden" is a rolling sequence of abstract thoughts and images. This song has nine stanzas, with no bridge separating them. Each stanza ends with a statement about the gates of Eden. In most cases, paradise is drawn as a contrast to life outside the gates. War, brutality, power, and materialism all characterize life on the outside of paradise. Is the final line, that "there are no truths outside of the Gates of Eden," a note of despair? In the last stanza, the singer is with his lover, so at least companionship exists. It may be that knowing of another possibility, even if it is locked away and unattainable, offers some sense of hope.

The introduction to this book made reference to Bruce Springsteen's howling lament, "Adam Raised a Cain." The song rages against the pain of sin and disappointment and raises haunting theological questions that have persisted down through the centuries. Lying at the center of the song is a son's struggle to come to grips with the life of his father. The hopeful image of baptism with which the song begins fades with the son's growing understanding of his father's pain and disappointment. The difficult world east of Eden, into which the first family is cast after the father's sin, is the location of Cain's own sin, the murder of Abel. The voice in the song agonizes over his own predicament. Weighty theological issues such as original sin and predestination are raised as the son realizes that his own life is shaped and determined by the sins of those who came before him. Even if we do not accept the idea that sin and its effects are biologically transmitted, it is all too plain that parental sins of addiction, bigotry, and abuse are passed on to the next generation. In more subtle ways, even weaknesses that might not be considered sins, such as fear of failure or poor health habits, might be passed on in this way. The final line of the song is too enigmatic to be a clear expression of hope. Can the dream of a parent to raise a child who is free from the forces that have bound previous generations be realized? The book of Genesis is also still working on this question when it comes to an end.

Jackson Browne's "Before the Deluge" appropriately brings this chapter to a close and points forward to the next. The biblical references are subtle but powerful. Browne's descriptions of those who lived before the flood resonates more with the genealogy of Cain than with the line that proceeds from Adam through Seth. Cain's genealogy would seem to represent progress and civilization in the ancient world. It speaks of building and metal working and music, all of which are captured in the first two verses of "Before the Deluge." What represents progress to some looks like destruction to others. The Cain genealogy of Genesis 4 and the Adam/Seth genealogy of Genesis 5 are not brought into contact in the biblical story, though it is fascinating how many of the same and similar names appear in both. The third verse of "Before the Deluge" raises questions about whether all human beings who lived before the flood were pleased with the direction of civilization. Can the sweeping generalization of Genesis 6:5, "and every inclination of the reckoning of his heart was only evil all of the day," really represent the experience of every human being? The tragedy of which the biblical text fails to provide even a glimpse is brought into view in Browne's words as "only a few survived."

Summary and Questions for Reflection

The stories in this earliest part of Genesis are part of the foundation of Western civilization. The provocative power of the images in these texts makes them ideal tools for the construction of poetry. At the same time, these stories raise the crucial issues and questions we confront in our lives. Here are some questions you might explore using the songs discussed in this chapter:

(1) Considering the metaphor of "moving east" as moving away from God, what in your life represents an eastward momentum taking you away from the being that created light, order, and goodness from darkness, emptiness, and chaos? What concrete steps can you take to reverse that momentum?

(2) Do you agree with the overall assertion that paradise and innocence are connected in some systemic and important way? If so, at what point in our lives are we most "innocent," and does that equate to the time in our lives when we are most God-like (*imago dei*)? Is it when we are born or when we die or somewhere in between? If it is when we are born, does the experience of life actually represent a de-maturing of the spirit?

(3) Considering the concept of naming the animals, is the process of naming things important to you? What is the importance of your own name? Is our ability as a species to formulate names and hierarchal structures of names important in our ability to make meaning out of life? How does the story's focus on the responsibility of humanity to give names to the rest of creation relate to our need for power and our ultimate sense of powerlessness in God's creation?

(4) The great power of Genesis lies in its clear establishment of relationship as a key issue to God and all of God's creation. From the beginning, nothing happens in a vacuum, and everything we do and every decision we make has implications beyond the moment, beyond our present circumstance. Do you find this concept overwhelming and unproductive? How do we focus on our immediate circle of influence while maintaining a balance with our impact on the larger world around us? Who does the most good in the world, the one who loves a few well or the one who loves the masses poorly?

(5) Sexuality is a powerful part of our human existence. It makes sense that it would be prevalent in all of our literature throughout the history of our species, and this part of the Genesis story is no exception. Do you think the focus on sexuality in the text is out of balance with life as a whole? Does the connection of sex to procreation outweigh its importance as a tool of intimacy? Do you feel the creation account is given for the purpose of establishing sexual norms within a godly society, or does the text use sexuality as one example of how God establishes expectations for the way we view and treat each other in all areas of life?

(6) The Emmylou Harris rendition of "Bang the Drum Slowly" (a song she co-wrote with Guy Clark) is a beautiful testimony to her love for her father and her deep sense of gratitude for his life and deep sense of loss in his death.

The Genesis story is deeply preoccupied with the beginning and ending of life. Would you be willing to write a lyric/poem of your own that expresses that level of appreciation for someone in your life whom you have lost? Would you be willing to allow others who share your memory of that person to see your writing?

(7) What other songs can you think of that have references to these biblical stories? What other questions came to mind as you were reading and discussing this section? If there was one concept or thought encountered in this part of the Bible that would cause you to live differently than you do now, what would it be and what will you do about it?

Notes

[1] The precise division of the two creation stories is in the middle of what is now numbered as verse 4 in chapter 2. This makes the naming of the two passages awkward. After this opening paragraph, we will refer to the stories using whole chapter numbers, Genesis 1 and Genesis 2.

[2] For a helpful discussion of the developing themes in the early chapters of Genesis, see David J. A. Clines, *The Theme of the Pentateuch*, 2nd ed. (Sheffield: Sheffield Academic Press, 2000), 66-84. For a further development of the relationship between Genesis 1 and Genesis 2, see Mark McEntire, *Dangerous Worlds: Living and Dying in Biblical Texts* (Macon GA: Smyth & Helwys, 2004), 18-19.

[3] See the brilliant and thorough discussion of the cultural development of these traditions in Elaine Pagels, *Adam, Eve, and the Serpent* (New York: Vintage Books, 1989).

[4] On the significance of eastward movement in Genesis, see Devora Steinmetz, *From Father to Son: Kinship, Conflict, and Continuity in Genesis* (Louisville: Westminster/John Knox, 1991), 89-91; and McEntire, *Dangerous Worlds*, 18.

[5] This is the helpful suggestion of Claus Westermann. See his *Genesis: A Practical Commentary* (Grand Rapids MI: Eerdmans, 1987), 32-33. For more on this idea of Abel's success in comparison to Cain, see Mark McEntire, *The Blood of Abel: The Violent Plot in the Hebrew Bible* (Macon GA: Mercer University Press, 1999), 20.

[6] For a fascinating discussion of the anti-technology and anti-city biases of the early chapters in Genesis, see Modupe Oduyoye, *The Sons of God and the Daughters of Men: An Afro-Asiatic Interpretation of Genesis 1–11* (Maryknoll NY: Orbis, 1984), 69-78.

CHAPTER TWO

Surviving the Storm

Singing about the Flood

The Biblical Texts

Genesis 6–9 tells the story of the flood and its immediate aftermath. The version of this story that resides in the awareness of popular culture is smoothed and sanitized. In contrast, these four chapters of the Bible present a story that is disjointed and perplexing in many ways. The first four verses of Genesis 6 are perhaps the most mystifying in the entire Bible. The story of the heavenly beings who procreate with human women and create a race of giants serves a number of purposes. It serves as one of those elements in the first eleven chapters of Genesis that reminds us we are in a different kind of world. It is a world where beings can move back and forth between heaven and earth, where giants roam, and where people live for many hundreds of years. The violence that began with Cain's killing of Abel has spiraled out of control, and God has reached the painful conclusion that creation needs a new start. The remainder of Genesis 6 describes God's choosing and instructing of Noah, the one selected to perpetuate the human race.

Genesis 7 describes the contents of the ark and the flood itself. It is easy to get lost in the confusing details about the number of animals taken on the ark and the duration of the flood and to miss the connections between the flood story and Genesis 1. The flood is an undoing of creation. In 1:6-8, God made the firmament, or dome, that arched upward separating the waters of chaos into waters above and waters below. In between was a livable space for the creatures of the land and sky, including human beings. This act of creation on the second day served to put the world in order and make subsequent acts possible. In 7:11, those waters from below erupt from "the fountains of the deep," and the waters from above pour through "the windows of the heavens." The "formless void" of Genesis 1:2 has returned, and creation is undone.

In Genesis 1:2, hope is provided in the midst of chaos by the spirit of God "hovering over the face of the waters." A parallel hope appears in 7:18 as the ark "went on the face of the waters." At this point, only in this box are the waters above separated from the waters below. It is the one seed left from creation, containing what is necessary for life to sprout forth again on the earth. In 8:1, God remembers Noah and the waters begin to subside. The world outside the ark begins to resemble what it was before, a livable space.[1] This space must be tested by sending out a raven and then sending out a dove three times. When the dove does not return the third time, the other inhabitants of the ark are able to leave, and they walk out into a new world.

Genesis 8:20-22 and 9:1-17 record two sequences of interaction between God and Noah. In both, God promises not to destroy creation in this way again. The covenant God makes with Noah is symbolized by the laying down of God's bow in the clouds. Though this certainly refers to the rainbow, it also means God has laid down the weapon of destruction and does not wish to make war against humanity anymore. The serene but brief portrait of peace and wholeness is immediately shattered in the perplexing story of Noah's sons in 9:18-27. It is not clear what happens in this story, but the result is human conflict and oppression. The flood does not resolve the antagonism between human beings.

Songs of the Flood

Noah is a figure that captures the imagination. The attention he gets rarely focuses on the building of the ark. Even in the biblical text, the building is not described. The ark itself is described in God's instructions to Noah in 6:14-16. The simple quotation in 6:22, "And Noah did, according to all which God commanded him, thus he did," leaves a great deal of artistic space. "Against the Grain," a song recorded by Garth Brooks, extols the maverick, non-conforming spirit. Noah is cited, along with Christopher Columbus and John Wayne, as an ideal example of this kind of spirit. The idea that Noah's friends and neighbors ridiculed him while he built the ark is one of those items completely absent from the Bible, though many people assume it is in the text. Nevertheless, the portrayal of Noah as a rebel in "Against the Grain" raises important theological issues. Genesis 6:8 says Noah "found favor" in the eyes of the LORD. It does not say whether this was because of Noah's superior moral behavior or simply because God needed to choose somebody to perpetuate the human race after the flood. The possibility that he is chosen because of his willingness to "buck the system" and "go out on a limb," as "Against the Grain" implies, is perhaps as good as any.

A song called "Flood" recorded by Jars of Clay takes a somewhat different perspective on the flood story. While the song is somewhat simplistic, it makes up for this shortcoming by assuming an unusual position. The reference to "forty days" undoubtedly links the song to the biblical flood, yet there is no mention of Noah or the ark. The voice singing the song is coming from the mud and is threatened with drowning. In most interpretations of the flood story, the people not on the ark are forgotten. Of course, the Bible pays them no attention either, once the rain starts. But one cannot help imagining the desperation of these drowning people. Michelangelo's painting in the Sistine chapel shows them struggling to climb on the ark, only to be beaten away with axes and clubs by young men, presumably Noah's sons. Jars of Clay's song allegorizes the flood to some extent, of course. It becomes the difficulties of life such as weakness, sin, and guilt, which threaten to swamp the singer. Thus the song becomes a lament, a plea to God from the singer to be rescued. In the flood story, such a prayer could not be answered, so what are we to make of it? One such prayer that is answered in the Bible is the one uttered by Jonah from the belly of the fish in Jonah 2.

A song called "Two Step," made popular by the Dave Matthews Band, makes a reference to the animals who survive the flood on Noah's ark. This is a primarily a love song, so it is not about the flood, but the repeated line in the refrain, "We're climbing two by two, to be sure these days continue," refers most specifically to Genesis 7:9, where the animals "went two by two unto Noah, unto the ark. . . ." The song "Two Step" recognizes that life passes quickly, that there is cause for celebration, and that companionship is a means of continuing life's goodness. Life is not all good, and there are "things we cannot change," but the singer promises his lover that their relationship will make "these days continue." Another possible reference to the biblical story of Noah appears in the middle of the song when the singer asserts that his lover is "like wine" to his mouth that has "grown tired of water all the time." Immediately after the flood, Genesis 9 reports that Noah planted the first vineyard and became the first winemaker. Though the flood brought destruction, it brought new creativity as well. This new creativity, though, is not without potential problems, as Noah's drunkenness initiates the conflict among his sons.

The end of the flood story may have captured the artistic imagination of great songwriters in a more significant way. Bob Dylan's "Blowin' in the Wind," made popular by its fabulous performance by Peter, Paul, and Mary, uses the image of the dove released by Noah after the flood. The bird sent out by Noah to survey the earth as the flood recedes is an irresistible image. The dove returns to the ark the first two times because it is not able to land on dry ground. The olive branch in its beak upon the second return indicates that progress is being made in the drying up of the earth. Only the third time it is sent out does the dove not return. "Blowin' in the Wind" is one of the great anti-war anthems of the Vietnam era in America. Amid the images of war and oppression, Dylan rightly sees the great flood as an act of war, which is confirmed by God's laying down of the bow at the end of the flood. The dove cannot land until the war is over. The dove and the olive branch have become symbols of peace, both separately and together. For "Blowin' in the Wind," however, peace is elusive, and the possibility of the dove resting is in question as long as "the cannon balls fly" and "people cry" without being heard.

Natalie Merchant's "Noah's Dove" is a much simpler song about a recollection of young romance. Noah's dove sees the purified earth for the first time, just as the singer's first lover experiences her innocence. She is the purified earth upon which he looks and lands. Unlike the dove, however, the lover does not choose to find a resting place. Instead, he is deceptive and "reckless." He chooses to see the relationship as confining and longs for the freedom of flight. The singer believes her lover has wasted a chance to find love, assuming that other chances will come along. Instead of the safety the dove finds on the ground, the lover prefers danger. So he chooses transience over permanence. For him the chaos of the flood may have just as well not ended.

Bono, the lead singer of U2, finally moves us out of the ark in "Beautiful Day." The song makes reference both to the dove with the olive leaf from Genesis 8:11 and the bow in the clouds in 9:13. It draws the contrast between a difficult and tortured life in an unnamed town and a vision of a more beautiful and peaceful existence. The two lines that draw on the flood story, "See the bird with a leaf in her mouth" and "After the flood all the colors came out," are in a sequence of short lines that portray contrasting images of beauty and ugliness. Geographical names and features, such as China, canyons, Bedouin, and oil fields, operate as a quick tour of the world. Creation and destruction are juxtaposed. The images of dove and rainbow end this sequence and carry the song to the final repetition of the chorus, which offers the alternative vision of a beautiful day, an escape from the confusion and loneliness of the demoralizing town that "You've been all over and it's been all over you."

Summary and Questions for Reflection

The biblical flood story offers powerful images of destruction and new creation. It is at once a personal story, with a hero named Noah, and a universal story of the undoing of creation. All major civilizations of the ancient Near East had their own version of such a story, and the biblical story shares many themes with the others. The struggle to survive both our own self-destructiveness and the dangers and heartbreaks the world hurls at us connects us to such a story. Here are questions to consider as you explore these songs.

(1) The contrast made between the "maverick" nature of Noah and the moral superiority of Noah and their possible connections to God's choice of Noah as a tool for regeneration of life on the earth is fascinating. Do you think God prefers mavericks (people who buck the system, who color outside the lines) to play the larger roles in God's great creation narrative? Considering that throughout the Bible, this rebellious nature is portrayed in both negative (Jonah) and positive (Jesus) ways, do you think this maverick nature that exists in all people to some extent is more sinful or sacrificial? Where would our species be without the great mavericks of years gone past who have taken us in entirely new directions in the areas of science, religion, culture, the arts, etc.? How does that compare to the importance of those who give consistency, stability, and permanence to our existence? Does the presence of this great continuum between the rebelliousness and the consistency in all of us say something about the complex character of God as well?

(2) The Jars of Clay song "The Flood" is a lament for God's help to rescue us all from the floods of life, both those created by our own doing and otherwise. Can you relate to the song? Are you drowning in life's complicated existence even as we speak? Can you relate more to the people on the ark watching helplessly as others go down? Does this song set up a false dichotomy that we are all either drowning or unable to help others who are? What is the middle ground in your own life, and how can you make real changes to help yourself and others through the real storms of life? Would you be willing to write a lyric/poem that expresses your own sense of drowning and share it with others in the group?

(3) The dove as a symbol of peace and new covenant between people has now become almost universal. But the powerful point in this chapter is that while God may have extended an olive branch to us, we have yet fully to extend it to each other. If the flood narrative is both a literary and literal foreshadowing of God's redemptive act within creation through Jesus, does this mean God will always intervene to save humanity? Are we capable of destroying ourselves still? Our current level of nuclear weapons deployment enables us to destroy our world several times over, and we are still seeking even more destructive technologies. Do you think the odds are greater that we will ultimately break God's cycle of redemptive action and completely destroy all life as we know it, or that we will find a way to bring God's redemptive model once again into the center of our relationships?

(4) If we take into account the presence of a flood narrative in so much of ancient literature, clearly this washing of the world is an old and common theme regardless of cultural heritage. Its presence in popular culture even today only reinforces its strength as a description of the human need to clean off the bad stuff to get a new start. Do you feel that we are fundamentally good at the core and that the bad stuff is layered on top and needs to be washed away? Or is it the other way around? Can you connect this issue in your discussion to the first half of this chapter and the issues raised surrounding the garden and the creation of humanity itself? Draw some connecting lines between this theme and the hymnody we use in our worship services that focus on the blood of Jesus as the washing agent in our lives ("Whiter than Snow," "Nothing but the Blood of Jesus," etc.). Discuss the metaphorical relationship that water is to the earth as blood is to the

body. Does this assume that the purest of washing always happens from the inside out and not the outside in? Could it be that the flood story represents God's admission that in the created order there are some things we must do for ourselves? Will God no longer "wash it all away" from the outside, but expect us to enter the discipline of internal, soulful cleansing that makes us better people one day at a time?

(5) What other songs can you think of that have references to these biblical stories? What other questions came to mind as you were reading and discussing this chapter? If there were one concept or thought encountered in this part of the Bible that would cause you to live differently, what would it be and what will you do about it?

Note

[1] For a thorough discussion of these themes in the flood narrative, see Walter Brueggemann, *Genesis*, Interpretation (Atlanta: John Knox Press, 1982), 77-87.

CHAPTER THREE

Family Matters

Singing about the Ancestors

The Biblical Texts

Beginning in Genesis 11:27, the biblical story narrows its focus to a particular family. A number of features serve to change the mode of storytelling in Genesis as Abraham, son of Terah, emerges as its first major character. In the first eleven chapters of Genesis, the characters are all flat. They have no developed personalities, and the stories about them are fragmentary. Abraham is the first highly developed character to appear in the biblical text. A well-connected series of stories about him allows the reader to discern many facets of his character—his hopes, his fears, and his dreams. The events also become quite different at this point in Genesis. The stories about Abraham and the other Israelite ancestors often involve the ordinary events of life rather than catastrophic floods and the building of great towers, and they take place at definite places. Beginning in Genesis 12, every event takes place at a location that can be identified on a map. These semi-nomadic ancestors of the Israelites would almost certainly have been recognizable to the first readers or hearers of the stories. They traveled to familiar places and they had recognizable lifestyles.[1]

Beginning in the stories of Abraham we find the notion of God making a covenant, or agreement, with a family. If Abraham agrees to go where God sends him and if he worships God faithfully, then God will provide Abraham with land, offspring, and prosperity. On the surface the stories of these ancestors seem relatively easy and simple, but careful reading reveals a difficult struggle to work out this new way of life lived in covenant with a new and mysterious divine being. Threats to this new way of life recur constantly as the story progresses. One of the most persistent threats is famine. Repeatedly, the ancestors have to leave the land of Canaan, which God has promised them, because its resources are insufficient to sustain their lives. Traveling in foreign territories puts their lives in jeopardy in many ways. Among other things, while traveling in another country, both Abraham and his son Isaac become afraid that they will be killed so that their wives can be taken. In order to prevent this, they both claim that their wives, Sarah and Rebekah, are their sisters. In three similar stories this deception creates a situation that has to be untangled, sometimes by divine intervention. The promises of the covenant are also regularly threatened by the difficulty some of the ancestral mothers have bearing children. The wives within these families and the children they produce are a source of conflict in many of the stories. This part of the book of Genesis seethes with sibling rivalry.

What is sometimes described as a "promise-threat-deliverance" pattern in the book of Genesis[2] reaches its peak in the story of the binding of Isaac in Genesis 22. The Hebrew word for "binding," *akedah*, is often used as a name for this story. Abraham and Sarah had struggled for years with childlessness. At an earlier point in the story, Abraham took Sarah's servant, Hagar, as a second wife and she gave birth to a son named Ishmael. Hagar's pregnancy and the birth of Ishmael caused conflict within the family, resulting in the expulsion of Hagar in Genesis 16. Hagar returned to the household of Abraham and Sarah and raised Ishmael there until Sarah finally gave birth to a son, Isaac, at an advanced point in her life. The birth of Isaac gives rise to additional conflict, this time resulting in the second expulsion of Hagar and Ishmael into the wilderness. This story in Genesis 21, in which Abraham endangers his son, Ishmael, is a mirror image of the story of the binding of Isaac in Genesis 22.[3] Both sons leave home with a parent by divine instruction. Ishmael and Isaac both reach the point of death, the former by thirst, the latter by a knife at his throat. In both cases, however, the parent looks up and sees something that saves the child. A well saves Ishmael in Genesis 21 and a ram in the bushes saves Isaac in Genesis 22. The stories both end with God speaking to the parent about the future.

The story of the binding of Isaac raises difficult issues, though. Just when the story finally seems to reach the place where it has wanted to go, and Abraham and Sarah have a child to continue the covenant line as God has promised, along come the horrifying words of Genesis 22:1, "Please take your son, your only one whom you love, Isaac, and go unto the land of Moriah, and offer him there for a burnt offering upon one of the mountains which I will say to you." According to the opening line of Genesis 22, God "tests" Abraham. We are not told why he needs to be tested. A brief dialogue between God and Abraham clarifies the command that Abraham is to offer Isaac as a sacrifice. Father and son travel along with servants to the foot of the mountain and then go up together, just "the two of them." At the moment when Abraham is about to strike his son with the knife, "the angel of the LORD" calls out and stops him. Abraham "lifts his eyes" and sees a ram in the bushes, just as Hagar lifted her eyes and saw the well in the previous chapter. He offers the ram as a sacrifice and the angel says, "Now I know that you fear God." The mood of this text is heavy and the cost of the test is high, as Abraham and Isaac now seem to be shadows of their former selves. Sarah, who is mysteriously absent in Genesis 22, dies in chapter 23. Abraham remarries and has more children, but his life and story have lost momentum. Isaac receives fairly brief attention, and his role in the text is little more than to be the father of Jacob, the next major character in Genesis. Thus, the story of the binding of Isaac is the climax of the Abraham/Sarah portion of the ancestral story.

There are two general ways out of the horrible conundrum of this text. One is that the voice Abraham hears is in his own head. God does not command him to kill his child, but he only thinks God has commanded him to do so, and God specifically intervenes to halt the killing. A second, related interpretation is that this experience is necessary for Abraham to discover that this God does not require the sacrifice of his firstborn son, a practice that may have been quite common at that time in the ancient Near East. Such interpretive efforts reveal the raw edge of this story and its ongoing power to wound readers. Perhaps we need to resist the temptation to find a resolution and instead leave this story as it is, with its jagged edge exposed.

As noted above, the story of Genesis passes by Isaac quickly to arrive at Jacob, the central character in the book. The many stories of Jacob revolve around two dramatic divine encounters in Genesis 28 and 32. We first meet Jacob as a young man in conflict with his older twin brother, Esau. In two separate accounts, Jacob takes first the birthright and then the blessing of the elder son from Esau. These events continue the theme of favor for the younger brother that began all the way back in the Cain and Abel story. Because of this conflict and the threat it poses to Jacob, he has to run away. He escapes from Esau by going north to the territory where the family of his mother, Rebekah, lives. His first divine encounter occurs as he is making the northward journey that will take him to the house of Laban, his uncle.

On the way, Jacob goes to sleep on the ground and has a dream. In the dream he sees a connection between heaven and earth. "Ladder" is the traditional translation of the word used to name this connection, but it could also be a stairway. Jacob sees "angels of God" going up and down the ladder, moving back and forth between heaven and earth. The account of this dream provides the occasion for God to recite to Jacob the covenant promises that had been made to Abraham and Isaac, his grandfather and father. The biblical text provides no interpretation of the dream other than Jacob's decision to rename the place "Bethel," which means "house of God." This story thus defines Jacob as the chosen one of his generation and establishes the importance of Bethel as a holy place.

Jacob's experience in the household of his uncle Laban (Gen 29–31), includes the acquisition of four wives, the birth of eleven sons and at least one daughter, and the accumulation of a large quantity of wealth, mostly in livestock. This part of his life is bracketed on either side by the account of the dream at Bethel and another, even more dramatic divine encounter reported in Genesis 32. In this scene, Jacob is traveling back toward his homeland, expecting to encounter Esau. In preparation for this reunion, he arranges his livestock and the human beings in his household so that he finds himself alone one night sleeping on the bank of the Jabbok River. Jacob is suddenly attacked by a being who is first described as "a man" but who takes on increasingly divine contours as the story progresses. The two figures wrestle to a draw, and as the sun begins to rise, they speak to each other. In the verbal exchange, Jacob receives a new name, "Israel," but the other being refuses to disclose his own name. This being escapes by injuring Jacob's hip. Jacob moves on with a limp, a new name, and the understanding that he has encountered God "face-to-face." In many ways the telling of this story matches its content. The wrestling match happens in the dark, and the ambiguity of the storytelling keeps the reader in the dark, unable to perceive exactly who is present and what is happening. Like we observed above with Abraham, in the aftermath of the binding of Isaac, Jacob continues to be the main character in Genesis, but his story reaches its climax in the wrestling match, and he is now merely transporting us, in limping fashion, to the next generation.

The basic storyline of Genesis is disrupted by the identification of Jacob as "Israel." If he is Israel, then all of his sons are "sons of Israel," and none can be rejected in favor of a chosen one. Still, the favoritism for the younger son persists. Joseph emerges quickly as the favorite son in Genesis 37. During the long period until the birth of Benjamin, he is the youngest son in the family. The favoritism shown to Joseph in the gift of the special coat[4] and his response to this favoritism in his report to the brothers about his dreams, leads immediately to conflict in the family. Joseph is sold into slavery by his brothers, who tell Jacob he is dead. The coat that signaled Jacob's favoritism for Joseph, soaked in animal blood, becomes the false signal of Joseph's death to Jacob. In the next chapter of Genesis, when Joseph resists the romantic advances of his Egyptian master's wife, he again loses his robe. This time the robe becomes the false signal of Joseph's guilt in the matter. Joseph's clothes and their removal are indicators of his decline from favorite son to slave to prisoner.

Joseph reaches bottom in Egypt when he is imprisoned, but his ability to interpret dreams becomes his salvation. He gets out of prison and into Pharaoh's house and eventually rises to the top of Egyptian society. His position as Pharaoh's chief administrator places him directly in the path of his brothers when the famine forces them to Egypt to find food. Ironies abound as the book of Genesis comes to a close. Jacob's favoritism and Joseph's arrogance fuel the jealousy of the older brothers. The result of this family conflict is that Joseph becomes a slave in Egypt. The same focus on dreams and their meaning enables Joseph to rise to the top, so that he is in a position to help his family when the famine comes to Canaan. No wonder that while forgiving his brothers in Genesis 50:20 Joseph says, "You devised evil against me. God devised it for good in order that doing so this day he might bring to life a great people." Nevertheless, all of these events make possible the ultimate enslavement of this great people, Israel, in the land of Egypt. The enslavement of the Israelites in Egypt, however, sets the scene for the central story of deliverance in Western tradition. The weaving interplay between evil intent and good result, between freedom and bondage, between suffering and deliverance creates a story that is boundless in its artistic and imaginative possibilities.

The final chapter of the book of Genesis accounts for the deaths of Jacob and Joseph. Before these deaths, Jacob recites a long poem about each of his twelve sons, or the tribes they represent. The song operates on two levels, just as the character known as both Jacob and Israel does. It speaks primarily of individuals in some cases. For example, in the section about Simeon and Levi, in 49:5-7, their murderous rampage in Genesis 34 seems to be the driving force. In other portions the poem seems more concerned with the future identity of the tribe, which takes on the name of the son. The portion about Judah in 49:8-12 primarily points forward to the future identity of the tribe as the source of the kings in the Davidic dynasty. The names of these sons of Jacob will be listed several more times in various ways in the Old Testament, and the order in which they are listed will fluctuate depending upon the purpose of the list and the shifting identities of the tribes.

Songs about the Ancestors

While Genesis 1–11 is packed full with texts that speak to the heights and depths of human existence, the stories of the ancestors pay much more attention to the ordinary aspects of human life. Thus, the places in the story that provide artistic power are more dispersed. In many ways the separate stories and sets of stories in Genesis 12–50 are all oriented toward their own focal points. All the struggles of Abraham and Sarah to survive in Canaan and to produce a family point toward the horrifying scene on Mount Moriah, where Isaac is bound, the knife is raised in Abraham's hand, and Sarah is far off, without a voice in the story.

At first glance, Joan Baez's "Isaac and Abraham" appears to be a short and simple poetic retelling of the *Akedah* story. However, the reversal of names in the title is an initial, subtle hint that something more profound is going on. The song embodies the wrenching efforts throughout Jewish and Christian history to come to terms with this painful and difficult text. The stark *a cappella* opening of the song creates an emotional mood that fits the grim reality of the story. The first stanza raises the question of the source of the voice Abraham hears. Is it a voice from outside himself telling him to kill his son, or something that comes from within? In the third stanza the conflict that has raged in Abraham's own head moves to heaven itself. The angels are weeping and questioning the decision to kill the "righteous boy."

Abraham's decision not to kill Isaac in the fourth stanza offers multiple understandings. Did he hear the objections of the angels from the third stanza? The direct statement of the "angel of the LORD" in the biblical text is not directly uttered in the song. Instead, there is an unexpected statement from Abraham expressing regret that he did not halt the sacrifice himself. Regardless of the source of the original inclination to kill Isaac, Abraham clearly acknowledges in this statement at the end of the fourth stanza that the decision not to kill him is prompted from outside himself. The praise directed toward Isaac in the final verse stands in contrast to the biblical text, which pays Isaac almost no direct attention at all. In the biblical tradition, the mountain on which this "binding" took place becomes connected to the holy hill of Zion, the future site of Solomon's temple. It is remembered as the place of Abraham's great act of faithfulness, but the song presents the mountain as a memorial to Isaac, and the puzzling reversal of names in the title of the song is resolved.

Bob Dylan's enigmatic classic, "Highway 61 Revisited," makes use of the *Akedah* story in a different way. The first verse presents a dialogue between Abraham and God, based on Genesis 22. In this dialogue Abraham objects to God's request to kill his son, and God must threaten Abraham in order to make him comply. The first verse ends without a resolution of the dispute between God and Abraham, but Abraham's inquiry about the location of the requested killing leads to the first reference to the Highway 61 in the song's title. Interpreters of this song have often pointed out that Dylan grew up near Highway 61 in Minnesota and that his father's name was Abraham, suggesting that there may be autobiographical elements in the song.[5] The remaining four verses each tell a fragmented story that is as difficult to comprehend as the first verse would be for a hearer who is not aware of the story in Genesis 22. Each story ends with a reference to Highway 61, linking it to the first verse. Little, if any, meaning and connection can be drawn from this collection of stories, and we should be hesitant to push too far to find them. The story of Abraham and Isaac does serve at the beginning of the song to establish Highway 61 as a location of human struggles, both internal and external. This place, like Abraham's Moriah, is the arena where hopes, fears, ambitions, dreams, and issues of life and death are negotiated.

The Grateful Dead's song "My Brother Esau" moves in and out of contact with the biblical story of Jacob and Esau. The song makes reference to an inheritance, parental favoritism, Jacob's dreaming, Esau's hairiness, and a blessing, all of which are elements of the Jacob-Esau saga in Genesis. The song speaks of Esau as one who goes to war and kills "the hunter, back in 1969." The time reference makes a connection to the Vietnam War most tempting. The line in the second verse, "my brother failed at war," may confirm this. The voice singing the song seems to be that of Jacob. He was apparently not in the war, but "the silent war it bloodied both our hands." So, in the song, Esau, the biblical hunter, embodies those who were sent to fight, and Jacob, whom Genesis calls "a quiet man, living in tents," does not. The conflict between these two groups then may be represented by the story of conflict between the two biblical brothers. In Genesis, Jacob and Esau are eventually reconciled when Jacob returns home. In the song, the reconciliation has not taken place, but Jacob has begun to think about Esau differently. In the final verse, he is asking questions about his own responsibility and the nature of the difference between his identity and Esau's. He ponders, "The more my brother looks like me, the more I understand." As the song ends, he also recognizes his brother's suffering as he imagines him "shadowboxing the apocalypse, wandering the land."

Bruce Hornsby's "Jacob's Ladder" is a relatively short and simple song that makes use of the famous dream of Jacob in Genesis 28. References to "salvation" and "angels" in the first verse immediately provide religious tones to the song. The two characters described in this verse, "the fan dancer" and the "fat man," are described as "fallen angels." The reference to "climbing Jacob's ladder" in the chorus that follows raises the possibility of redemption from this fallen state, but seems to insist that such redemption is a long climb, "step-by-step," in contrast to the "in-hand salvation" being sold by the fat man. The second verse makes more explicit reference to a television or radio preacher. Again, there is a promise of easy salvation. This salvation is coupled with sending money to the preacher, of course. The first-person voice in the song responds this time, claiming satisfaction with a gradual, daily improvement. The final line from this verse, which hopes only for a tomorrow that is "better than today," is repeated one more time before a final rendition of the chorus about Jacob's ladder. In Genesis 28, Jacob is clearly on the bottom rung as he flees for his life with nothing. He is at the beginning of a long climb that will lead him to his status as Israel's namesake. Thus, this song, with its repudiation of easy, instant salvation, fits the text to which it refers. The long, difficult struggle of Jacob is pulled into the song alongside the striving of its characters.

"Bullet the Blue Sky," a U2 song from 1987, opens with imagery from the crucifixion. The song is filled with flashes of uncertain images that match the sound of the song. Among these images is a reference to Jacob's wrestling match in Genesis 32. The timing of this song and some of its images evoke the turmoil of Central America in the mid-1980s. According to the song, Jacob wrestled with an angel "and the angel was overcome." There are problems with this interpretation on two major points. First, the text never says Jacob wrestled an angel, and, second, the match seems to be a draw rather than a victory for Jacob. Such misinterpretation may be deliberate, of course. "Bullet the Blue Sky" sounds like a critique of American imperialism. Is Jacob, the cheater and usurper, being linked with frequent, covert American attempts to control this region of the world? Is America the great protector, as the final verse suggests, or is this a deceit? The reading of Genesis 32 that lies behind this song may be problematic, but the elements of fear, turmoil, uncertainty, and threat to identity connect the song's lyrics intimately with the text. Jacob is blessed by the being with whom he wrestles, but he also walks away limping, wounded by the encounter. Blessing and attack may be difficult to distinguish. U2 raises serious questions in "Bullet the Blue Sky" about what those who would use military power to "deliver" others are truly accomplishing.

An entirely different interaction of the Old Testament and music can be found in the musical stage play by Andrew Lloyd Webber and Tim Rice called *Joseph and the Amazing Technicolor Dreamcoat*. The soundtrack of the play also became a hit album. In many ways, this musical retells the story of Joseph from Genesis 37–50. The format of the show and the music itself, however, fit with many of the most popular musicals of the late 1960s and early 1970s. Joseph is the grand hero at the center of the play, which ponders what it means to rise and fall, to be captive and to be free. The soundtrack contains twenty-two songs, some longer and some shorter, and they all relate to the biblical text in some way. It would be impossible to discuss all of them here. An important song called "Jacob and Sons" is sung near the beginning of the play. One of the things this song accomplishes is the introduction of the characters. Singing about the twelve sons of Jacob is not without precedent, because Jacob himself sings such a song in Genesis 49. In Genesis, however, the twelve sons have already been introduced in the stories of their births, mostly in Genesis 30. The song from the musical alludes to the dual identities of Jacob and his sons as characters in Genesis. Jacob has been renamed Israel, and the text of Genesis sometimes calls him by that name, reminding us that he represents a whole nation. The song reminds us, though, with the line "most of the time his wives and sons just called him

Dad," that Jacob is also an ordinary character. Likewise, the sons operate on two levels, as individuals in the story and as the names of the future twelve tribes of Israel. The song also reveals the maneuvering of these names by abandoning the birth order at the end in order to list Joseph last, as the favorite. Genesis 49 stays with the birth order of the sons as recorded earlier, but the many lists of the twelve sons and tribes that appear subsequently in the Old Testament will play with the order in the list as the status of tribes rises and falls. Rice and Webber have captured the complicated family dynamics in the story and the theological dynamics of its significance in the larger story of Israel.

Dolly Parton's "Coat of Many Colors" plays with many of the themes of the Joseph story, but often reverses them or turns them on their heads. The coat she remembers as a child is a symbol to her of her mother's love. Gender has been reversed in the song, making this a mother-daughter rather than father-son story. Parton comes from a large family, but siblings are never mentioned in this song. The choice to ignore the issue of favoritism in the song can be maddening, but it wants to place the focus of the conflict elsewhere. One also might wonder why a mother would link this coat to the Joseph story, when the coat nearly gets Joseph killed and helps lead to his enslavement. The song seems to block out these troubling issues in favor of others. While one gets a sense in the biblical story that Jacob's family is wealthy and that Joseph's coat is luxurious, perhaps almost royal in appearance, Parton's "Coat of Many Colors" wants to speak about poverty and love. Taunting classmates replace the jealous brothers. The song invites the hearer to consider whether their teasing is born of a similar jealousy. In the biblical story, the good and bad that come with Joseph's coat are all experiences that help form him and shape his life. This is an idea that Joseph himself embraces in Genesis 50:20. In the song, Parton goes "wondering once again back to the seasons of my youth." It is clear that both the love of her mother, sewn into the coat, and the reaction of the other children, regardless of their motivation, have similarly shaped her life. Despite the frustrating incongruities between the biblical text and the song, they manage to raise many of the same questions.

The story of Jacob's family forms the end of the book of Genesis and points forward to the book of Exodus. In Genesis 12, Abram and Sarai go to Egypt because of a famine, and Sarai is held captive, in a sense, in Pharaoh's house. Joseph has spent time as a slave in Egypt and, though he and his family are not slaves at the end of Genesis, they are in their eventual place of slavery. These interlocking themes of the Joseph story and the exodus narratives that follow are on full display in Bob Marley's classic "Redemption Song." The freewheeling poetry of the song is not always easy to follow. It seems to weave older worlds ("pirates") and more modern ones ("atomic energy"). Like Joseph, the singer has been in a pit, has been sold into slavery, and has had his hand strengthened "by the hand of the almighty." Literal slavery may not be an overt part of the world to which Marley is singing, but he is painfully aware of the "mental slavery" that still afflicts his audience, along with the approximation of slavery that is created by poverty, whether in his native Jamaica or the larger world to which he ultimately sang. In a way that fits well with the biblical tradition, Marley believes music and poetry are a means of achieving freedom. The Israelites sing their first "song of freedom" just two chapters after their liberation when Miriam and Moses lead them in the "Song of the Sea" in Exodus 15. Like the book of Genesis, though, "Redemption Song" ends with the fate of its protagonist still hanging in the balance. Has his song fully emancipated him?

Summary and Questions for Reflection

Jacob's mysterious wrestling match in Genesis 32 forms the center of this first book of the Bible. Through this struggle he acquires and recognizes his purpose and identity. This achievement requires fierce determination, and it can exact great cost. When it is over, Jacob knows things he did not know before, but he also leaves wounded. Our own identities are tied up in issues of family, work, spirituality, and suffering. Finding true identity requires a willingness to accept the rewards and pain that come with it. The characters and stories of Genesis are a resource that can supply us with the energy and imagination this struggle requires. Here are some questions to consider as you encounter these stories and listen to the songs of others who have encountered them.

(1) We have raised the issue of covenant between God and the family of Abraham. How would you define the word "covenant" based on that relationship? If you had to define a covenant between God and your family, what would that look like? Who initiated it? Who were its original parties— your parents, your grandparents, you and your immediate family group, however that is composed? Has God kept God's side of the covenant? Have you kept yours? How might you understand the consequences of successes and failures in keeping covenant?

(2) The near sacrifice of Isaac by Abraham is a horrifying story. Discussion of the biblical text above points out two traditional interpretations of the story as readers throughout history have struggled to make sense of something so painful and bizarre. Could you offer another? In your own life, what would take a command from a divine being to sacrifice, good or bad? The Joan Baez song "Isaac and Abraham" moves Isaac to the center of the story and lifts him up as the true hero. Have you ever felt that God or somebody else is sacrificing you on the altar of life? To what or whom do you attribute your deliverance?

(3) It has been said that everyone is addicted to something. Only the drug of choice and the intensity of the compulsion differ. If that is so, what drug of choice is causing you problems in life? Equate your struggle in this area to Bruce Hornsby's interpretation of Jacob's struggle (or perhaps his own?) in "Jacob's Ladder." What is the offer of "easy salvation," and who is the "fat man" that keeps prolonging your suffering by providing temporary relief to your problems? Do you see how that stands in the way of doing the hard work necessary for more substantive and long-term healing in your life? Talk about how people might look at the bottom and top of the ladder if the metaphor represents our struggle to become the free and mature people God has called us to be.

(4) The concept of a "coat of many colors" has been used extensively throughout literature and the arts since its conception in the Genesis story of Joseph. Its power comes both from our yearning for someone to acknowledge us as important enough to separate us from the rest as well as its focus on our basic needs of covering and shelter. Can you recall acts of love on the part of others that have met these needs in your life? Can you pinpoint a metaphorical "coat of many colors" someone gave to you that made you feel special and unique in the world? What part are you doing to be the giver of that coat to others?

(5) Are familiar with the phrase "No good deed goes unpunished"? That cycle of good deeds having bad consequences and vice versa is all through these great stories in the book of Geneses (see the treatment on Joseph). Can you identify times in your life when what appeared to be a blessing had negative consequences? Can you identify times when things that looked terrible and painful on the front end yielded God's grace and love in tangible ways

over time? How might that enable you to be forgiving to those who had good intentions toward you in the past but created painful results? How might that enable you to forgive yourself when you meant well with an action or a gift toward others but things did not turn out as you had planned?

(6) In what sense do you understand your life and its consequences to be larger than you as an individual? Does the "Song of Jacob" in Genesis 49 imply that the character formed in the lives of individuals is passed on to those who come after them? Does our individualistic society take away all emphasis on collective identity? How does the Andrew Lloyd Webber and Tim Rice song "Jacob and Sons" (and the whole *Joseph and the Amazing Technicolor Dreamcoat* musical) help you think about collective identity and its consequences?

(7) What other songs can you think of that have references to these biblical stories? What other questions came to mind as you were reading and discussing this chapter? If there were one concept or thought encountered in this part of the Bible that would cause you to live and be differently than you are now, what would it be and what will you do about it?

Notes

[1] For a more complete discussion of these themes and literary features in Genesis, see John H. Tullock and Mark McEntire, *The Old Testament Story*, 7th ed. (Upper Saddle River NJ: Prentice Hall, 2004).

[2] On the problems and possibilities of describing general themes in Genesis, see David J. A. Clines, *The Theme of the Pentateuch*, 2nd ed. (Sheffield: Sheffield Academic Press, 2000); and Joseph Blenkinsopp, *The Pentateuch: An Introduction to the First Five Books of the Bible* (New York: Doubleday, 1992), 109-11.

[3] The story in which Hagar and Ishmael are banished into the wilderness (Gen 21:8-21) has apparently been moved out of its natural chronological position to be juxtaposed with the story of the binding of Isaac in Genesis 22. These two stories in which the two sons of Abraham are threatened have numerous common elements. Note the narrative incongruities in 21:14-15, where Ishmael, approximately fifteen years old at this point in the larger story, is placed on Hagar's shoulders and thrown under a bush like an infant. Chronologically, the story would fit better back in the area of Genesis 16, soon after Ishmael is born, but chronology is not the determining force in the narrative here. For further discussion of the relationship between these two stories and the shape of the book of Genesis, see Mark McEntire, *Dangerous Worlds: Living and Dying in Biblical Texts* (Macon GA: Smyth & Helwys, 2004), 24-25.

[4] The traditional rendering, "coat of many colors," is primarily a guess. The meaning of the Hebrew word used to describe the coat is uncertain. A more recent translation, "coat with long sleeves," is also not much more than a guess.

[5] See the discussion of this song in Michael J. Gilmour, *Tangled Up in the Bible: Bob Dylan and Scripture* (New York: Continuum, 2004), 3.

CHAPTER FOUR

Let Me Out

Singing about the Exodus

The Biblical Texts

Understanding texts in the book of Exodus requires a vision of this book as a whole. The composition of Exodus is a more complicated matter than that of Genesis. The book falls fairly naturally into two halves, but the relationship of the two halves is difficult to describe. Exodus 1–18 tells a story that begins with the identification of the Hebrew people in Egypt and ends with them arriving at Mount Sinai, in the wilderness, after they have escaped from slavery. The force that most effectively holds the book of Exodus together is the gigantic personality of Moses. He is both the driving force of the narrative and the great lawgiver.[1] Of course, the exodus event continues beyond the book that has taken the word "Exodus" as its name. The primary ideas and characters developed in this book extend through the end of the book of Deuteronomy, when Moses gazes out across the promised land from the top of Mount Nebo just before his death.

Moses is introduced as an infant in Exodus 2. Ironically, he is thrown into the Nile, just as Pharaoh had commanded his people to do with all

Hebrew baby boys in 1:22, but this act saves him rather than kills him. This kind of irony will recur frequently in the story of Moses. Moses is saved because of the "basket" his mother makes for him. The Hebrew word for this container is the same as the word used to name the "ark" Noah builds. Moses survives the chaotic threat of water in his little ark, just like Noah and his family survive in their larger one. Within just a few verses after this event, Moses has grown up, murdered an Egyptian taskmaster, and fled into the wilderness. By the end of Exodus 2 he is married to a Midianite woman named Zipporah and has a son of his own named Gershom.

At this point, the text slows the narrative significantly in order to present two monumental encounters between Moses and God. The best known of these encounters begins with Moses' observation of a bush that is on fire but is not being consumed. The "burning bush" episode of Exodus 3 takes on great significance because Moses is selected by God to lead the Israelites out of slavery in Egypt, and he discovers his purpose. Moses' meeting with God comes while he is performing shepherding duties for his father-in-law. This and many other aspects of the story in Exodus 2–3 serve to transform Moses from a fugitive Egyptian prince to a semi-nomadic sheep herder who looks a lot like Jacob, the ideal Israelite. The burning bush encounter perhaps corresponds most closely to Jacob's dream at Bethel. During this encounter the identity and name of God are revealed to Moses and he is given miraculous powers. Remember that the being who wrestled with Jacob refused to reveal his name in Genesis 32:29. So, when the divine name is revealed to Moses in Exodus 3:14, Moses surpasses Jacob. In 4:2 we are told that Moses has a staff in his hand. This ordinary object, a tool of hikers and shepherds, will become an object of mystery and magic that will initiate plagues in Egypt and great acts of deliverance in the wilderness for the Israelites.

Moses' first attempt to free the Israelites from slavery in Egypt fails, requiring a second encounter with God in Exodus 6. This second meeting and the commands God gives to Moses propel the story back to Egypt, where the thrilling and horrifying story of the plagues occurs. This is a point in the story where we become acutely aware that it is being reported to us from a particular point of view, an Israelite point of view. This story surely looks quite different from an Egyptian perspective. Readers of the plague narratives have struggled for millennia with two troubling aspects of the story. First, the text tells us repeatedly that God will "harden Pharaoh's heart," beginning in 4:21. God seems determined to prolong and magnify the conflict with Pharaoh. Second, innocent Egyptians, children included, suffer in the plagues. "Collateral damage" is a modern label placed on an ancient reality. Innocent ones suffer while the mighty struggle for power. The African proverb describing this reality says, "When two elephants fight, the grass gets hurt." We might wish that the book of Exodus was more explicit in raising questions about the injustice of this reality, but it does not flinch from observing it.

The brutality of the plague narratives reaches its pinnacle in the tenth and final plague, the killing of all the firstborn of Egypt, which is linked to the Passover tradition in Exodus 12. The report of this event is provided in three ways. In 12:1-20 God gives instructions to Moses concerning the Passover and the killing of the firstborn. In 12:21-27 Moses passes on the instructions to the Israelites, and 12:28-32 narrates the events of that night. It is in 12:23 that the theological turmoil brewing behind this story comes to the surface. Here it is not God who actually enters houses to kill children in the night, but a mysterious "destroyer" who is under God's command. God is thus kept at a distance from the actual killing.[2] Nevertheless, the Egyptian children and livestock are dead, and Pharaoh himself cries out in grief, his heart no longer hard.

With the Egyptians paralyzed by the wrenching grief that follows the final plague, the Israelites finally burst forth in freedom into the wilderness. Very quickly, however, Pharaoh and his court recover from the devastating blow, and they decide to pursue the Israelites. This decision sets up a final showdown between Moses and Pharaoh, when Pharaoh's army traps the Israelites on the banks of the Red Sea at 14:9. The story of the deliverance at the sea is depicted twice in Exodus. A prose account of the event fills much of Exodus 14, and a poetic account, commonly called the "Song of the Sea," is presented in Exodus 15. Even in ancient times, this is the kind of event about which Israel seems compelled to sing. They are free from Pharaoh, but what are they free for? The remainder of the Pentateuch will struggle to answer this challenging question.

The idea of a "promised land" was born in Genesis 12:1 when God called Abraham to leave his home and "go to a land which I will show you." The common phrase "land flowing with milk and honey" appears first in Exodus 3:17. The actual phrase "promised land" does not appear in most English translations of the Bible,[3] yet the ideal of a promised land to which God will lead the Israelites becomes pervasive beginning in the early parts of the book of Exodus. Throughout the book of Exodus, and the rest of the Pentateuch, this image serves as the goal toward which the Israelites are moving. It is also a key element of the covenant God makes with the Israelites to provide them with a new way of life after they leave Egypt.

Another important part of this covenant is the various sets of laws given to Moses by God throughout the remainder of the Pentateuch. This complex and difficult portion of the Bible is easy for modern readers to ignore, even though it provides the first five books with one of their collective names, the "Law." Ancient rabbinic tradition delineates 613 distinct commandments in this material, governing everything from personal behavior to livestock management to the celebration of festivals. In a modern context, much of this material seems irrelevant. Readers need to be careful, however, not fall into the easy habit of pulling small pieces of the material out of context and applying them to modern life. The legal material in Exodus through Deuteronomy appears to consist of a number of different law codes that come from different periods in Israel's history. They have been pieced together in a way that is difficult to follow and often seems contradictory.[4] It is perplexing, for example, that much of Exodus 21 is concerned with the regulation of slavery, since this is a set of laws given to a group of people that has just escaped from slavery and is struggling for survival in the wilderness. One particular law, from this same chapter, that receives a great deal of attention is the famous "law of retaliation" in Exodus 21:23-25. This law governs harm brought about in a fight between Israelites. Any harm shall be repaid "life for life, eye for eye, tooth for tooth, hand for hand, foot for foot." This law represents the great conundrum for Christians and Christian communities in addressing the law because it is specifically overturned by Jesus in Matthew 5:38-39, when he commands his followers to "turn the other cheek." Has Jesus overturned only a few of the laws, or has he provided a model for overturning all of them? This question is made even more difficult by Jesus' perplexing statement in Matthew 5:17-18, "Do not think I have come to abolish the Law or the Prophets. I have not come to abolish but to fulfill. Truly, therefore, I tell you, until heaven and earth pass away, a small letter or a stroke of a letter will not pass away from the Law until all is accomplished."

Living in the wilderness presents immediate problems for the Israelites. By definition, the wilderness is a place that cannot sustain life on a permanent basis. The harsh nature of the wilderness sets up a tension in the book of Exodus between order and disorder. The memory of the reliability of life in Egypt frequently beckons the Israelites to return to a life of slavery, as in 17:1-4 when the people cry out with thirst in the wilderness. The opposite pole of the disordered wilderness is the order of law offered to the Israelites through Moses at Mount Sinai. Much of the legal portion of Exodus, chapters 20–40, is concerned with the construction of the tabernacle and its equipment. The centerpiece of this portable worship center is the ark of the covenant. In Exodus 25:10-22 God gives Moses instructions for the building of the ark. In 37:1-9, a craftsman named Bezalel uses these instructions. Both texts describe a cover for the ark, which is commonly called the "mercy seat" in English translations. This helps to highlight the dual function of the ark as both a container for the tablets of the law and as God's throne. From this point forward, the Israelites carry the ark with them, and it becomes a key element of the holy war tradition, by which they are commanded to take possession of the promised land. The careful ordering of law and of the space and materials in the tabernacle balance the chaotic experience of living in the wilderness.

Beyond Sinai, the Israelites begin another perilous stage of their pilgrimage from Egypt to the promised land. The text and the Israelites sit still from Exodus 19 to Numbers 10, while Moses moves up and down the mountain, struggling to maintain a connection between Israel and God. In Numbers 10, the Israelites move back into the wilderness on a journey specifically designed to kill off all the adults counted in the census at the beginning of the book of Numbers, and the harsh landscape of the wilderness is up to the task. The Israelites do battle with this terrifying environment and they do battle with God, as Moses tries to intervene. They finally come to rest again on the Plains of Moab at the end of the book of Numbers. The book of Deuteronomy consists primarily of speeches of Moses given to the Israelites in this place. The Jordan Valley and its river are all that lie between the Israelites and the land of Canaan at this point. In the final chapter of Deuteronomy, Moses gazes across that river and sees the promised land. At this point, the promised land is not yet a reality, but it is the dream of an ordered and productive existence that stands in contrast to the threat of chaos in the wilderness. In Moses' vision from the mountain, the land is already divided up by tribes with established borders and boundaries that heighten this dream of order and stability. The Law is boxed up in the ark of the covenant, and the worship life of Israel is packed away with the tabernacle, both ready to be opened to provide the order necessary for a permanent and productive existence. Moses dies on Mount Nebo following this vision, and it will be left to Joshua and the remaining Israelites to cross over into the promised land and attempt to live in that vision.

Songs of Exodus

The burning bush Moses encounters in the wilderness, which leads to his first of many divine encounters, has become a symbol for momentous or transforming events. The well-known R.E.M. song "Man on the Moon" is ostensibly about the comedian Andy Kaufman. The innovative nature and strangeness of Kaufman's comedy created a cult following. Like many such figures, a sense of mystery surrounds his death, and there are speculations that he may still be alive—hence the connections with Elvis Presley and conspiracy theories about lunar exploration in the song. A sense of mystery also surrounds the story of the death of Moses in Deuteronomy 34, but the more overt connection between this song and the Bible is the line "Moses went walking with a staff of wood." Along with the accompanying references to Newton, Cleopatra, and Darwin, the brief allusion to Moses' journey in the wilderness evokes aspects of mystery, discovery, and deliverance. The view of the song is enlarged beyond the life of Andy Kaufman to raise questions about what it means to take risks, to be innovative, and to be thought peculiar. The line that appears in the next verse, "Here's a truck stop instead of Saint Peter's," hints that something wonderful might be found in the ordinary, or even the annoying. Moses did not go looking for God. He was just tending his sheep in an ordinary place and suddenly saw something unexpected.

The burning bush encountered by Moses is also an image incorporated into the song "Standing Still" by Jewel. This is a relatively simple song whose most obvious reference is to a romantic relationship. As is typical in many songs, it is a troubled relationship. The singer seems confused and uncertain, raising constant questions about her own feelings and the feelings of the other person in the relationship. The questions imply a need to make a choice about the relationship. The burning bush is on the singer's right and a "dead end" on the left. In the story in Exodus 3, Moses must turn aside to look at the burning bush. In the song, the singer seems lost, and it is not clear whether she is prepared to turn aside to see the burning bush. The song ends with the singer still uncertain about her direction and destination. This is a good reminder that while the burning bush episode is a turning point in the life of Moses, it is only the beginning of a quest. He leaves the divine encounter with a significant sense of uncertainty about his own sense of purpose and must return just a few chapters later to talk with God about the experience of failure he has in Egypt.

It is fitting that perhaps the most honest, artistic description of the horror of the final plague comes in a heavy-metal package in Metallica's "Creeping Death."[5] The voice of this song is that of the "destroyer" from Exodus 12:23, who aptly identifies himself, "I'm creeping death." The song plunges us into the anguish of the story. How can a people enslaved for 400 years be set free? The destroyer pleads his case that "something must be done." He justifies his acts of death with the claim "I'm sent here by the chosen one." Like the story in Exodus itself, the song attempts to place distance between God and the direct act of killing. References to other events in Exodus—the burning bush, the turning of the Nile to blood, and the plague of hail—fill the center of the song, but it soon returns to that night filled with death. The burden of this task is evident in the voice of the singer. Even the single line acknowledging the deliverance of the Israelites from this plague by the lamb's blood placed on their doorposts does not alter the heaviness of the mood. Before deliverance can be celebrated, its horrible cost must be acknowledged. The repeated refrain of the song proclaims that the writing down of this story perpetuates its meaning and maintains the identity of the force that commits this horrible deed, "creeping death."

Though the final plague would seem to be the winning stroke in the struggle between Moses and Pharaoh, the pursuit of the Israelites into the wilderness by the Egyptian army sets up one more conflict and one more act of deliverance. The miraculous rescue of the Israelites at the Red Sea is a monumental event that is central to the identity of the Israelites. This powerful symbol of deliverance plays a key role in a song by Patty Griffin, which is simply called "Moses." The actual sea the Israelites cross in Exodus 14–15 becomes, in the song, a metaphor for a difficult emotional experience from which the singer must be delivered. Specifically, the sea is the loneliness caused by a broken relationship. The enormity of the emotional pain is depicted as something that only Moses, the great deliverer, can overcome. An interesting addition to the refrain is the further identification of the "sea of loneliness" as a "red river of pain." This line seems to conflate two other biblical events, one on either side of the deliverance at the sea. The first is the initial plague produced by God through Moses that turns the Nile River red in Exodus 7:14-25. The other is the crossing of the Jordan River in Joshua 3–4, a story in which Joshua causes the flow of the river to stop so the Israelites can cross into Canaan on dry ground. This additional line thus piles up images of power over water. Water is the Bible's ultimate image of chaos. God's power over water, through Moses at the Red Sea and on other occasions, becomes a powerful indicator of God's ability to deliver people.

Once the Israelites arrive at Mount Sinai in Exodus 19, the story comes to a near halt while Moses receives and delivers the law. It is not surprising that the legal material that fills most of Exodus through Deuteronomy is not a frequent source of images and ideas for songs. There are some useful words and images in these texts, though, and a song like "The Mercy Seat" by Nick Cave makes interesting use of some of them.[6] "Mercy seat" is a common translation of the word used to designate the ark of the covenant, or its cover, which Moses instructs Bezalel to make in Exodus 37. This song is sung from the perspective of a death-row inmate. It begins with a catalogue of strange and disturbing images and visions, as the prisoner waits for the "mercy seat." This cover of the ark, which also functions as a symbolic throne for God, is eventually equated with the electric chair that will bring death to the prisoner. About one-third of the way into the song this becomes clear when he climbs into the mercy seat with his head shaved and his "head is wired." The song moves back and forth between images of death and deliverance. The prisoner seems both to yearn for and dread the finality the seat offers. Religious language and imagery abound as the song continues. The ark is envisioned in heaven as the throne of God, the center from which "all history does unfold." This heavenly, golden throne is contrasted with the earthly chair of "wood and wire" in which "my body is on fire." The prisoner also struggles with the guilt of the crime that has brought him to this place. Another familiar phrase from Exodus 21:24, "an eye for an eye and a tooth for a tooth," appears frequently. This phrase, known as the "law of retaliation," is a familiar expression for punishment that fits the crime. In the song it is the result of "all this measuring of the truth," and marks the finality of the prisoner's fate. The final phrase of the chorus, "I'm not afraid to die," is repeated each time the chorus appears, until it changes in the final chorus to "But I'm afraid I told a lie." The singer finally confronts his fear of death, and the song ends on this haunting note.

The familiar "eye for an eye" line also occurs in a song called "Crossfire," made popular by Stevie Ray Vaughn. This is a song about economic hardship in which the singer needs to beg and steal in order to survive. He is asking to be rescued or treated with kindness, but continues to realize in each repetition of the refrain that "We're stranded, caught in a crossfire." This song raises a question inherent in the exodus story. Can one person or group of people be delivered without another being damaged or destroyed? Must the Egyptians be killed in order to save the Israelites? Must the Canaanites lose their land so that the Israelites can gain it? Is all of life a "zero-sum" game? It is interesting that "Crossfire" also makes reference to Jesus' command to "turn the other cheek" in Matthew 5:38-39. Jesus makes this statement as a response to the law of retaliation from Exodus 21. The final verse of "Crossfire" claims that this simply does not happen, that in order to survive one must be strong and not trust anybody. This is the brutal world in which the singer is "stranded," and the final words of the song cry out in despair, "Help me."

It is not surprising that the "promised land" would appear frequently in songs as an image of hope for the future. Bruce Springsteen's "Promised Land" is a mixture of exhilaration and frustration. The singer is a mechanic by day who races his car at night. He expresses frustration in the grind of his daily work and seems to realize that the excitement of racing is a "mirage." This leaves him longing for change and feeling like he is going to "explode." Destruction looms both inside of him and off in the distance. The inner doom makes him want to "Take a knife and cut this pain from my heart," while the external threat is a "dark cloud rising" and a "twister to blow everything down." Despite all of the fear and turmoil, the song returns repeatedly to the image of the "promised land" in the chorus. Yet this portrait of hope seems distant and unattainable. The song reaches no resolution as the despair of the singer and his hope for the future balance each other precariously. Throughout the Israelites' journey in the wilderness, the promised land loomed in the distance, sometimes only as a dim hope. The wilderness was filled with danger, however, and many did not survive the journey

The "promised land" motif appears again in Billy Joel's "River of Dreams," a song brimming with religious imagery. The song points ahead to the Jordan River, which the Israelites will have to cross to enter the promised land. The river is portrayed as a barrier and accompanies other topographical images, such as "mountains of faith" and "valley of fear," which are common in religious language and form a part of the exodus/wilderness experience for the Israelites.[7] The singer walks in his sleep and sees these images in a dream, searching for a lost sense of spirituality. The land on the other side of the river represents the thing he is searching for. Weariness and the threat of death hang over the singer. Whether it is deliberate or not, this gazing across the river at the promised land evokes the life of Moses. Moses dies without crossing the river. In the song, it is uncertain whether the singer gets across. He "wades in" the river in the final verse, but a later line says "we all end in the ocean." This might be taken as a failure to cross, but it might also be understood as an affirmation of community. Moses, as an individual, never crossed the Jordan River, but he was a part of the Israelite people who did make it to the other side. The closing lines indicate that perhaps the river itself is the ultimate destination.

One final, striking image of the "promised land" idea appears in John Mellencamp's harsh protest song, "Rain on the Scarecrow." This song emerged from the era that witnessed the collapse of many small farms in the United States in the mid 1980s. These sentiments were the catalyst for the "Farm Aid" movement and the concert series in which Mellencamp was a driving force. "Rain on the Scarecrow" pleads the case of the Midwestern farmer who has been crushed by large economic forces and faces foreclosure. Religious images fill the middle of the song as the singer recalls his grand-mother sitting on the front porch of the farmhouse holding her Bible. The rich, fertile Midwest had been like a promised land to the millions of people who settled there, but the promise of the place has been disappearing. The earlier refrain "Rain on the scarecrow, blood on the plow" becomes even bloodier after the failure of the farm as "There'll be blood on the scarecrow and blood on the plow." In the first line of the song, the scarecrow had been mounted on a "wooden cross." Only when the local courthouse yard becomes filled with "ninety-seven crosses" representing ninety-seven lost family farms is it clear that the scarecrow has been crucified. The image of the promised land has failed, and the grandmother singing "Take me to the promised land" may be singing only of a heavenly deliverance. The song ends with a father apologizing to his son that the promised land is now only a memory, not a hope for the future.

A fitting end to a discussion of songs about the exodus might be found in the grand Bob Marley anthem by that name. Marley's music was focused on the lives and religious experiences of his people of Jamaica, who were descendents of slaves, so it is only right that his first big hit on the interna-tional stage was one that connected their experience to the exodus story. Marley's "Exodus" has the scattered abstract feel characteristic of reggae music, but repeated lines hold it together. "Movement of Jah people" is the dominant line. Here, he uses the pronounceable first half of the unpro-nounceable name of God revealed to Moses at the burning bush. Because of physical danger, Marley had left Jamaica shortly before he recorded this song, urging his listeners to "Open your eyes and look within." The movement he advocates is not so much a physical journey as a mental and spiritual one.

The captivity of poverty and oppression are labeled as "Babylon," and Marley cries out to God to "Send us another brother Moses." He calls not only for the people to move, but also for Jah to come and "break down oppression" and "set the captives free." The song ends with multiple repetitions of the line urging a movement of the people to accompany or even instigate the movement of God.

Summary and Questions for Reflection

The second through fifth books of the Bible, Exodus through Deuteronomy, begin and end with Moses. While this gigantic figure is the center that holds these books together, they are hardly a biography of Moses. The grand tensions of life are juxtaposed in this sweeping story—freedom and captivity, order and chaos, stability and uncertainty, security and danger, life and death. The choices between these tensions are not easy. Egypt represents ultimate order and certainty, but it is also a place of captivity. The wilderness is a place of freedom, but it also holds danger and death. The legal tradition of the Old Testament stands at the center, offering a sense of order, but the law contains a great deal of death. Here are some questions to think and talk about as you explore these songs that reflect elements of the story of the exodus.

(1) We have identified the rich and complex irony found in the story of Moses as he is "thrown" into the Nile as commanded by Pharaoh. This act actually serves as his salvation, and we see the great connection made by the same Hebrew word being used for Moses' basket as is used for Noah's ark. How do you view this event in the narrative? Is it a redemptive act of God? Is it the work of the characters in the story acting on their own accord? Is it merely providence or a random act of luck? Can you name an event in your life that should have been your downfall but that yielded a "salvation" experience instead? How do you interpret that experience in light of this narrative?

(2) The difficult representation of God as a being that engages in acts that have dire repercussions on innocent people (especially children) is probably more visible in this part of the Bible than any other. How does your personal theology process a God that seems to "harden the heart of Pharaoh" in an effort to prolong the conflict? Is it perhaps an issue of perception by the Hebrew writers that is actually a misconception about God's activity in the

story? If not, how do you reconcile that God with the God of Jesus who is repeatedly shown in the Gospels to be a great lover and protector of children?

(3) The wilderness in which the Israelites wander as they proceed to the developing vision of a "promised land" is a harsh and difficult place. For many, it seems to represent the painful parts of life we often have to go through to get to something better on the other side. When you hear that statement, how does it make you feel about God and God's creation? Do you agree or disagree with it? Can good things come to us without times of long suffering? Other interpretations understand the wilderness experience not as the difficult stage that leads to better times, but as the necessary in-between time that separates the violent and degrading time of slavery from the emancipation of the promised land. Do you agree more with that interpretation? Why? Still other readings view the wilderness experience as an ideal time when the trappings of civilization do not intrude on the divine-human relationship. Is this more consistent with your own experience?

(4) Many of the songs we have highlighted here offer in creative form stark and vivid feelings of disruption and confusion in life. Can you relate to this perspective? Can you cite times in life when you were really trying to do what you thought God wanted you to do, only to encounter failure and fear at every turn? How did it turn out in the long run? Looking back, do you still feel you were following the will of God? Is confusion and difficult decision-making inherent with being God's children in the world? What would it mean to decide that you had misinterpreted God's direction in the past?

(5) The overarching theme of emancipation taken from the exodus account has been one of most powerful metaphors ever portrayed in artistic form. Its presence in the collective consciousness of the human spirit has carried entire groups of people through unbelievable times of pain and suffering. Would you be willing to create your own form of expression for this universal theme—perhaps a poem, a short story, a song, a picture, a dance, a dedicated time of personal weeping followed by celebration for all of the times God has performed this miracle of emancipation in your own life? Would you be willing to share it with your closest friends and family?

(6) Do you remember the assertion that water is the Bible's ultimate image of chaos? What does water mean to you? Can you understand how it can have such power in this narrative and yet also have a redemptive and cleansing quality in other parts of the Bible? Systems theory has taught us that a certain amount of chaotic behavior is actually an important part of the evolutionary processes of our lives. Can you talk with others about how chaos and redemption can be two sides of the same coin? Our Lutheran friends talk a lot about remembering one's baptism as an anchor for one's spirituality and sense of calling both from and to God. What part does water and baptism play in your own spiritual journey?

(7) Consider the presence of Moses in this great epic. Does God always require monumental leadership to accomplish redemption and emancipation on a grand scale? Many of the songs in this chapter deal with ordinary people in ordinary circumstances that carry their own sense of difficulty. These ordinary experiences may be easier to relate to than grand, epic adventures. Can you see Moses in that light? How did this ordinary man become an extraordinary leader when life's circumstances demanded it? While few if any of us are called to do that kind of thing on that grand of a scale, can you identify areas of your own life where you can do the small things that make a big difference in the life of someone else? What holds you back? What would help you move forward?

(8) What other songs can you think of that have references to these biblical stories? What other questions came to mind as you were reading and discussing this chapter? If there were one concept or thought encountered in this part of the Bible that would cause you to live differently than you are living now, what would it be and what will you do about it?

Notes

[1] See the discussion of the size and influence of Moses' character, both within the Bible and in other cultural adaptations, in Melanie J. Wright, *Moses in America: The Cultural Uses of Biblical Narrative* (Oxford: Oxford University Press, 2003), 65-68.

[2] For a fuller treatment of this text and the theological issues surrounding the Passover event depicted in Exodus 12, see Mark McEntire, *The Blood of Abel: The Violent Plot in the Hebrew Bible* (Macon GA: Mercer University Press, 1999), 49-60.

[3] Though the Hebrew Bible does not have a specific phrase equivalent to "promised land," some English versions have used this phrase to translate various Hebrew words and phrases. The New Living Bible, for example, uses the phrase about ten times, beginning in Exodus 13:17.

[4] For a more thorough discussion of the various law codes and how they compare in content and form, see John H. Tullock and Mark McEntire, *The Old Testament Story*, 7th ed. (Upper Saddle River NJ: Prentice Hall, 2004), 82-87.

[5] See the discussion of this song and others by Metallica from a religious perspective in Paul Martens, "Metallica and the God that Failed: An Unfinished Tragedy in Three Acts," in *Call Me the Seeker: Listening to Religion in Popular Music*, ed. Michael J. Gilmour (New York: Continuum, 2005), 95-114.

[6] The religious aspects of Nick Cave's music are the subject of a marvelous essay that does not discuss "Mercy Seat" specifically. See Anna Kessler, "Faith, Doubt, and the Imagination: Nick Cave on the Divine-Human Encounter," in *Call Me the Seeker*, 79-94. Some discussion of this song is included in J. R. C. Cousland, "God, the Bad, and the Ugly: The Vi(t)a Negativa of Nick Cave and P. J. Harvey," in *Call Me the Seeker*, 129-57.

[7] For a beautiful and insightful discussion of how the features of our natural environment and our faith help shape each other, see Simon Shama, *Landscape and Memory* (New York: Vintage Books, 1995), 245-67.

CHAPTER FIVE

The High and Mighty

Singing about Warriors, Kings, and Queens

The Biblical Texts

The Pentateuch ends with the death of Moses in Deuteronomy 34. The following set of books in the Bible, Joshua through Kings, is often called the Deuteronomistic History. These books tell the continuing story of the Israelites in a way that closely fits the ideology of Deuteronomy. This is a vast and sweeping story that covers six or seven centuries. Typical ways of reading this part of the Bible and the use of its contents in popular music have tended to focus on some of the colorful characters. While characters are the focus here, we will also try to pay attention to the connections between these characters and their larger stories.

Though the book of Joshua is named for its central character, Joshua himself is not an instantly captivating character. The book goes to great lengths in its first five chapters to portray him as a new Moses. He speaks to the Israelites like Moses in Joshua 1. He sends spies into Jericho in chapter 2, just like Moses sent spies into Canaan in the book of Numbers. In Joshua 3–4, he leads the Israelites miraculously across the Jordan River in a scene reminiscent of the crossing of the sea under the direction of Moses. Joshua even has a mysterious divine encounter in chapter 5 in which he is told to remove his shoes "for the place which you are standing upon is holy" (5:15). These words are identical to those Moses heard from the burning bush in Exodus 3:5. Yet Joshua never becomes a fully developed character like Moses. Instead, his life and character become linked almost entirely to a single event, the battle of Jericho. Everything else leads up to it and then flows out of it. The story of this battle appears in Joshua 6 and plays a vital role in the book.

Joshua 13–22 contains the long and tedious account of the allotment of the promised land, tribe by tribe and clan by clan. To make this allotment possible, the land must be taken from its Canaanite inhabitants. The story of the battle of Jericho stands at the beginning of this process and functions as the ideal victory, the model of how holy war is supposed to work. Careful reading, however, reveals cracks in the ideal picture. The goal of eradicating the temptations of Canaanite culture by killing everyone and burning everything is disrupted by the rescue of Rahab and her family and the collection of the metal objects that cannot be burned. The jubilation of the victory is tempered by Joshua's pronouncement of a curse on Jericho and anyone who attempts to inhabit it. Why have they conquered it? In essence, the story is told three times—in God's instructions to Joshua (6:2-5), in Joshua's instructions to the Israelites, and in the narrator's description of the events.[1] These last two versions of the story are intertwined in 6:6-27. All of the elements of holy war are present—a sanctified army, the ark of the covenant, the priests with their trumpets, the great shout, and the ban of destruction against the enemies and their property. This last element, however, also contains the seed of failure.

In the story of the battle of Ai in Joshua 7, we discover that one Israelite, Achan (Trouble) has kept some of the precious metal objects from Jericho as loot. The battle of Ai is the model story of defeat, standing in opposition to the battle of Jericho. Once Achan is identified as the cause of the trouble and he and his family are executed, the Israelites are able to attack Ai again and are successful. The story of the battle of Ai, again in direct contrast to the battle of Jericho, is virtually absent from popular memory and imagination. After Ai, the battle stories in the book of Joshua get progressively shorter until chapter 12 becomes merely a list of defeated Canaanite kings. Joshua 13:2 reveals that this story of the "conquest" of Canaan has nothing to do with reality, but such a conquest must be at least imagined before the land can be parceled out and assigned.

The book of Judges quickly descends into the gritty reality of life in Canaan for the Israelites. It is not possible to kill everybody, and it is not possible to live a life completely unaffected by the surrounding culture. We might even object to the overt ideology of the book of Joshua, deciding that neither of these are worthy or desirable goals. Without a clear central character or linear purpose, though, the book of Judges struggles with how to proceed and tell its story. Beginning in Judges 2, it falls into an uneasy cyclical pattern that presents six characters in succession who are often identified as the "major" judges—Othniel, Ehud, Deborah, Gideon, Jephthah, and Samson. The cycle of idolatry, defeat, oppression, and cry for help leads to the identification of each of the judges as a deliverer raised up by God to rescue the Israelites from their enemies. In the stories of the first three of these judges, military success leads to the overthrow of the oppressors followed by a lengthy period of freedom and peace until the judge dies. These measured successes fade, however, as the sequence moves toward its end in Samson. Samson's birth is recorded in some detail in Judges 13. It includes the dedication of Samson as a Nazirite, a commitment that includes not cutting his hair. Samson marries a Philistine woman who is eventually taken away from him. This leads to his violent confrontations with the Philistines and, eventually, to the death of his wife and her father by burning. After this, Samson falls in love with Delilah, who eventually discovers that his strength is the result of his Nazirite vow not to cut his hair. Delilah is either forced through fear or coerced with money to extract and report Samson's secret. When she cuts his hair, he is captured, has his eyes gouged out, and is taken to a Philistine house or palace where he is tied to the pillars. The story of Samson comes to a close in Judges 16 when he prays for strength one last time so he can pull the house down on top of himself and his captors.

Ironically, as the periods of peace in the book of Judges get shorter, the stories about the judges become longer and more interesting. The character of the judges declines, but their characterization in the narrative becomes richer and more fully developed.[2] The result is that the worst of the judges, Samson, becomes the most celebrated, and tradition tries to turn him into a hero—often succeeding through selective reading of the biblical texts.

The story of Samson leads the book of Judges into a sequence of chaotic and horrifying stories that fills its final five chapters. The brutal rape and dismemberment of the Levite's concubine in Judges 19 stands at the center of this sequence and eventually leads to civil war among the Israelite tribes. Framing this terrible set of stories is the repeated statement in 17:6 and 21:25: "In those days there was not a king in Israel. Each did the right in his own eyes." The first half of this statement is also inserted at 18:1 and 19:1 as a reminder of the perceived problem and the proposed solution. This refrain propels the biblical story forward into the books of Samuel and Kings, which will introduce us to the monarchy in general and some of the kings in particular.

The certitude about the moral character of kingship with which Judges ends will give way to great ambiguity in the book of Samuel. The Samuel character seems to offer initial hope that the tradition of the judges might be revived, but even the Song of Hannah, sung by Samuel's mother in 1 Samuel 2:1-10 at his birth, points forward to the monarchy (v. 10). The devastating defeat of the Israelite army at the hand of the Philistines in 1 Samuel 4 ignites the desire for a king among the people. First Samuel 8 brilliantly portrays the three-way negotiations among Samuel, the people, and God. The people get what they want, a king to "go before us and fight our battles," but Samuel gets to pronounce the devastating cost of such a bargain in 8:11-18. Samuel's description of an abusive king sounds much like Solomon to those who might have read ahead in the story, but for the time being, Samuel's ill will and harsh judgment fall entirely on Israel's first king, Saul. The failures of Saul, whether they are his fault or the result of Samuel's manipulations, set the stage for Israel's greatest king.[3] By 1 Samuel 16, Samuel is secretly anointing a new king, David, who is still only a boy. This anointing of David as king means God's spirit is now upon him and raises questions about the status of Saul, who is still very much alive. In intriguing fashion, 16:14 reports that "The spirit of the LORD abandoned Saul, and an evil spirit from the LORD tormented him." David is brought in to ease this torment with music. These encounters become confrontations between spirits, and the evil spirit departs, but David also earns his reputation as a musician that will extend into a long tradition of David as the Bible's great psalmist.

This story of David's first appearance in the palace is followed, somewhat mysteriously, by one of the most well-known tales of David, his battle with Goliath. The story is convoluted and does not easily fit into its context. The David who became a palace fixture in the previous chapter and was described as a great warrior is now an unknown boy in 1 Samuel 17. Nevertheless, in thrilling fashion, young David challenges and defeats the great Philistine champion with sling and stone in a duel filled with prancing and trash-talking. David's fame grows quickly among the Israelite populace, but the result of David's popularity is a growing jealousy in Saul. The conflict created by the love-hate relationship between Saul and David fills the remainder of 1 Samuel, until Saul dies in the final chapter.[4] The David and Goliath story is further complicated by the distant acknowledgement in 2 Samuel 21:19 that a warrior named Elhanan killed Goliath. Recognition of this claim might lead readers to ask serious questions about the story. Is it pro-David propaganda? Is it a hero story that spun out of control? Why does the writer of the book of Samuel let us in on this secret?

David is a figure of great contrasts, though. Standing in opposition to the great warrior/king/poet figure is David the adulterer and murderer. David's image reaches such a high altitude by the time he consolidates the Israelite monarchy, establishes Jerusalem as his capital, and expands Israel's territory to its greatest limits in 2 Samuel 10 that it may have nowhere to go but down in the stories that follow. Second Samuel 11 begins the story of David's decline by describing his affair with Bathsheba and the subsequent murder of her husband, Uriah. This event unhinges David and his family, leading to rebellion and internecine strife up to the point of David's death when two of his remaining sons, Adonijah and Solomon, are struggling for the throne.

The Old Testament contains two versions of the story of the Israelite monarchy, one in the books of Samuel and Kings and the other in the book of Chronicles. Chronicles is a retelling of Israel's story that begins with Adam, the first man. It uses nine chapters of genealogy to compress all of Genesis through 1 Samuel into a small space. Many great figures in Israel's history appear only as a single name in these genealogies. The purpose of Chronicles is to reach the stories of David and Solomon as fast as possible and to present them in a revised and glorified manner. David's affair with Bathsheba is not mentioned, nor are the murderous struggles for the throne in which David and Solomon engage. The inclusion of Samuel, Kings, and Chronicles in the Old Testament results in an enigmatic, multidimensional picture of the two greatest kings in Israel's history.

None of these books, however, presents an entirely positive portrait of the monarchy as a whole. Both versions of the monarchy describe the division of Israel into two kingdoms, ruled by two different kings, after the death of Solomon. This is a long tale filled with a few good kings and many evil ones, and the general picture is of the decline of the Israelite monarchy until surrounding empires destroy it. In 2 Kings the ultimate example of an evil king is Ahab, king of the northern nation of Israel. Ahab is most often remembered for his marriage to the Phoenician princess, Jezebel. Beginning with Solomon, the Israelite kings apparently joined in the common ancient

Near Eastern practice of exchanging daughters with foreign kings as wives to seal alliances. Israelite prophets often condemned this practice because these foreign wives brought foreign ways, including their own gods, into Israelite society. Behind this theological argument lay the general suspicion of women, especially foreign women, who are sometimes depicted or interpreted as temptresses in the biblical tradition. In the history of biblical interpretation, Jezebel is the temptress of all temptresses. Her story spans much of the book of Kings, from her marriage to Ahab in 1 Kings 16:31 to the report of her death in 2 Kings 9:33-37. She is a powerful narrative figure who overshadows her husband and becomes a worthy foe to the great prophet, Elijah.

Two stories of Jezebel most aptly demonstrate her character from the perspective of the biblical writer. Elijah appears as a prophet in 1 Kings 17. He immediately comes into conflict with Ahab over the worship of Baal, which is linked to Jezebel's influence. This conflict leads to the great contest between Elijah and the priests of Baal on Mount Carmel in 1 Kings 18. A great burnt offering is prepared on top of the mountain. The priests of Baal prove unable to call down fire from heaven to ignite the altar, but Elijah is able to perform this miracle. The priests of Baal are suddenly seized and killed in the aftermath of the contest. When Jezebel hears that the priests she sponsors have been slaughtered, she responds with an attack on the prophets of Israel, and Elijah is forced to flee for his life.

Jezebel appears again in 1 Kings 21 when King Ahab is attempting to enlarge his landholdings around the palace, but has failed to acquire the adjoining vineyard of a man named Naboth. When Jezebel hears of Naboth's refusal to sell his property to her husband, she conspires to have Naboth falsely convicted of a crime and executed. She acquires the property and gives it to her husband. Elijah reappears at this point and confronts Ahab, condemning Ahab and Jezebel to a death like Naboth's. The dogs will lick up Ahab's blood (21:19), and the dogs will eat Jezebel (21:23). Though Ahab repents at this point, he is eventually killed in battle, and when they wash his blood off his chariot, the dogs come and lick it up (22:35) as Elijah had proclaimed. The death of Jezebel comes much later, long after Elijah himself has ascended into heaven. In 2 Kings 9:33-37 she is thrown from a window into the street where she is trampled by horses and eaten by dogs.

Eventually, the northern kingdom of Israel is destroyed by the Assyrian Empire, and the sins of rulers like Ahab and Jezebel are blamed for the demise of the nation. In similar fashion, the southern kingdom of Judah is overrun by the Babylonian empire about a century and a half later. Again the destruction is portrayed as punishment for Israel's disobedience, especially that of its royal leaders.

As mentioned earlier, the book of Chronicles retells the story of the Israelite monarchy. While Chronicles removes much of the content of the story in Samuel and Kings, it often adds lengthy lists of various kinds. Chronicles is enamored with the priesthood, and many of these lists focus on priestly assignments. Eventually, the story in Chronicles reaches the same end, however, as powerful empires destroy the kingdoms of both Judah and Israel.

Songs about Heroes and Villains

"Ramble on Rose" is a fairly abstract song, typical of the Grateful Dead, that draws in fragmented and familiar images and figures, from Jack and Jill to Billy Sunday to Mary Shelley's Frankenstein. The first verse mentions just the name of the city, Jericho, with a reference to "walls" in the following line. That quickly and easily, the full story of the battle of Jericho is drawn into the collage. While it is hard to say precisely what this song is about, the images seem to focus on things gone wrong and dreams unfulfilled. One's perception of the battle of Jericho depends, of course, on one's position and identity. For most of the citizens of Jericho, it means death. Rahab and her family are spared, but their home and way of life are destroyed. The Israelites win a battle but seem to gain little in the process. The reality of life in the promised land never matches the imagined ideal, and "Ramble on Rose" arrives at the conclusion that "The grass ain't greener, the wine ain't sweeter, either side of the hill."

Like a powerful magnet, the story of Samson and Delilah has grabbed the attention of many songwriters. Barry Mason and Les Reed wrote "Delilah," the song made famous by the equally magnetic Welsh pop singer, Tom Jones, for whom the song became a signature. Tension abounds in the biblical story in Judges 16, and this tension persists for modern hearers, not least in the contrast between our popular perception of this "wicked temptress" and the pleasing sound of her name. The story in the song is not a precise parallel to the one in the Bible, but both are told from the perspective of a man who has been deceived by a woman. In the song the woman is unfaithful with another man, while in the Bible Delilah participates in the Philistine plot to capture Samson. In the song the man who is singing kills Delilah out of jealousy, but the Bible does not inform us explicitly of

Delilah's ultimate fate. It may be most natural to assume that she is killed along with Samson and his Philistine captors when he causes the collapse of the house in 16:26-27. If so, then Samson kills her. The most intriguing parallel between the text and the song lies in their afterlives. In each one, the tragedy, fueled by jealousy, anger, and envy, is covered up in a celebration of the characters. Samson becomes a folk hero in biblical interpretation, and Delilah becomes an object of longing in the repeated singing of the song.

The deception inherent in the Samson and Delilah story and its violent, destructive end are often overlooked when these two characters become the paradigmatic illicit lovers. The raucous "Sin Wagon" by the Dixie Chicks is sung from the point of view of a woman who has been in an abusive and oppressive relationship. Her husband/boyfriend has lived a life of freedom while she has been the dutiful wife/girlfriend. When she finally decides to break free and enjoy the pleasures of sin, she describes herself as "Delilah lookin' for Samson." The biblical story tells us Samson loved Delilah (Judg 16:4), but does not tell us how she felt about him. We only know that she betrayed him for money, though we are not sure if she had the power to choose another alternative. Delilah is, therefore, one of the few women in the Bible who exercises a measure of control over the men around her. The singer in "Sin Wagon" seems aware of the short-term ("I don't know where I'll be crashin'") and long-term ("That's if he forgives me") consequences of her actions, but she cannot resist the longing to control rather than be controlled.

Samson and Delilah can also play a role in what seems to be a more positive romantic song, like Bruce Springsteen's "Fire," performed most memorably by the Pointer Sisters. The song was originally written in the voice of a man expressing the intensity of his feelings for the woman he is with and trying to convince her that she should feel the same. He believes she is denying her feelings for him, and, as the song approaches its end, Samson and Delilah appear, along with Romeo and Juliet, as picturesque examples of romantic couples that inhabit and enliven the imagination of modern popular culture. The inclusion of Samson and Delilah may undermine the song's determination to some extent, since the biblical story seems to imply that her feelings did not match his. Are hearers of this song supposed to recall that both of these famous love affairs ended in suicide? The power of romantic love in this song obscures its destructive possibilities.

There seems to be some question concerning who wrote "Samson and Delilah," a song performed and recorded often by the Grateful Dead. Rather than pulling the image of Samson and Delilah into a somewhat unrelated song, like the other examples above, this song is a retelling of some of the events in Samson's life, including his ill-fated love affair with Delilah. A clue to the song's purpose may be the line that begins and ends it: "If I had my way, I would tear this old building down." Our last glimpse of Samson in Judges 16 comes as he is pulling down the Philistine house to which he has been bound. In one last feat of strength, he pulls the house down and is killed along with the Philistines. This song recalls Samson's love for Delilah, his slaughtering of a Philistine army with a donkey's jawbone, and his killing of a lion, but the tragic end of his life brackets and overshadows all of these events. In the first half of the book of Judges, Othniel, Ehud, and Deborah live long, full lives and die in peace. The frustration of this song accentuates the role of Samson, upon whom not just a building but the whole traditional "period of the judges" collapsed.

Leonard Cohen's "Hallelujah" exists in many different versions performed by many different singers.[5] It is a song nearly as big and complex as the biblical character who plays a major role in it, King David. The opening verse of the song seems to refer to the story in 1 Samuel 16, when David is brought to the court of King Saul to play his lyre and soothe the mad king. Samuel had secretly anointed David as the next king, so the spirit of God that rests with the king is upon him, and "an evil spirit from the LORD" torments Saul. When David comes to play for Saul, the spirit David possesses drives the evil spirit away from Saul. The opening verse also seems to refer to the tradition of David as the great composer of psalms.[6] Already there is a hint, though, that this relationship between David and God, which is like music, is not simple. David is, according to Cohen, "the baffled king composing Hallelujah." The second verse of the song then launches into the story of David's affair with Bathsheba. Cohen also appears to pull in a fragment of the Samson and Delilah story with his reference to the cutting of hair. The result of David's affair in the song is that "from your lips she drew the hallelujah." The utterance of this illicit hallelujah is a turning point in the song, and the next verse confronts the taking of the name of the LORD "in vain." There have now become two hallelujahs, one "holy" and one "broken." The final verse holds out the hope of redemption, however. Somehow, David's reputation as a faithful king survives all of his missteps in the biblical story, including the affair and the resulting murder of Uriah. Cohen's song switches to first-person voice in the final stanza, apparently portraying David's own words as he struggles to reclaim his connection to

God and the meaning of his holy "hallelujah." This attempt to rewrite a failed story with claims of "I did my best" and "I've told the truth" fits the long tradition within Judaism and Christianity of remaking David that began with the cleansing of his image in the book of Chronicles.

Fewer popular songs than one might imagine make use of the David and Goliath story and of the image of the giant-killer that produces many references in other types of popular expression, such as sports broadcasting. A song called "Cumbersome," performed by Seven Mary Three, makes an enigmatic reference to David and Goliath. In popular thought and conversation, Goliath has come to represent the prohibitive favorite in any kind of contest. As such, he has become a symbol of power, pride, and arrogance. The David of this story represents the underdog, filled with youthful exuberance, lightness of being, and the courage to stand up to power. The voice in "Cumbersome" is a man singing about a relationship with a woman in which he has taken on something of the character of both of these figures. In her eyes he seems to be transforming into Goliath, so that any David-like qualities have become a "mask." The result of this transformation is that his presence has become burdensome to her, heavy like the presence of an armored giant. The song uses the image of stones being thrown that accumulate and build a wall of separation. The singer longs for renewal of the relationship, but it moves inexorably from the lightness of being represented by David to the painful heaviness represented by Goliath. The final verse argues that there might be a proper "balance" between these qualities of lightness and heaviness, but such balance seems irretrievably lost.

The "temptress" tradition in the Bible begins with Eve, travels through the stories of Delilah and Bathsheba, and reaches its pinnacle with Jezebel, the Phoenician princess whom Ahab, ruler of the northern kingdom of Israel, marries. Popular music has also seized Jezebel and the resources she supplies as the instant image of a wicked woman. In Chely Wright's hit song "Jezebel," the wicked queen represents another woman with whom the singer is competing for the affections of a man. The Bible does not depict Jezebel as a seductress. The marriage of Jezebel to King Ahab of Israel, in 1 Kings 16:31, is likely a political arrangement, but it leads to increased worship of Baal, a rival god, in Israel. The Bible's Jezebel turns out to be a tenacious and fiercely loyal figure. She defends her husband against his opponents and detractors, especially the prophet Elijah. The line in the chorus of the song, "I will fight for love until the death," is appropriate if the other woman is anything like Jezebel. She outwits and murders many people in promoting her husband's purposes, and she long outlives him. Her own life ends in violent fashion, though, in 2 Kings 9:33-37, when she is trampled by horses and eaten by dogs. The woman whose voice sings this song has produced a formidable image of her opponent by linking her to the ancient queen.

Natalie Merchant made significantly different use of this famous temptress image in her song called "Jezebel." The woman who sings this song seems to be in a marriage that has become severely strained. She struggles with her changing feelings about the relationship and uses the name Jezebel to label herself and these shifting emotions. She has a desire to leave her husband and is overwhelmed by the sense that she is betraying him, unlike the biblical Jezebel who was fiercely loyal to her husband, whatever her motives may have been. The Jezebel of popular tradition has absorbed even more bad qualities than the biblical character possesses. The opening line of the second verse, "You lie there, an innocent baby," implies an image of this woman awake in the night while her husband sleeps. She rehearses the words she needs to say to him, fearful of the pain they will cause. The last two verses serve to make it unclear whether this is a permanent death of love, leading to a broken relationship, or an honest struggle with the natural ways love evolves as a relationship matures. The singer obviously still cares deeply for her husband, but her romantic feelings are not the same as they once were. The final lines reveal a need for honest communication. A simplistic view of marriage has blinded both of them to the complexities of human emotions and relationships. A simplistic view of Jezebel as temptress also blinds most readers to the complexity of this character and the stories about her in the Bible.

The song titled "Kenaniah," recorded by the band Petra, extracts one of the obscure names from a list-like section of Chronicles and develops a more complex image of this person. First Chronicles 15 tells the story of David bringing the Ark of the Covenant to Jerusalem. The story includes a list of priestly duties. 15:22 says, "Kenaniah, the leader of the Levites in singing led the singing because he understood." This character is understandably a fascinating one for songwriters and musicians. He may represent one of the earliest professional musicians mentioned by name. The context of 1 Chronicles 15 seems to be misunderstood in this song, which portrays the scene as one of battle. By the time David brought the ark to Jerusalem, it was no longer being used as an instrument of war. The song wishes to remember Kenaniah and to continue the tradition of singing to God that he began long ago. Whether deliberately or not, the line "Kenaniah, Kenaniah, we will lift it to the sky" captures the enigmatic meaning of the word in 15:22 often translated as "music," "singing," or "song," a word having something to do with "lifting up."

Summary and Questions for Reflection

The fascinating characters that fill the Deuteronomistic History are often the subject of Bible stories for children. They have become ingrained within the fabric of popular culture so that their names alone evoke powerful images— Joshua, Samson, Delilah, David, Goliath, Jezebel. While these are tremendous figures in the biblical narrative, they seem to grow even larger as they move through time. They may become interesting mirrors in which to look as we examine our own lives. Here are some questions to consider as you explore these songs.

(1) The story of Joshua and the battle of Jericho is one of the most well-known stories in the Bible. But step back from the story for a minute and read it again as if you are reading for the first time. Can you appreciate the issues raised in this chapter about the purpose of the battle and the questions concerning its ultimate success? Can you read the story from the perspective of the Canaanites? Can you relate the plight of the Canaanites to a contemporary people such as the Native American Indian in our country? Write a journal entry for an imaginary diary as if you were different people in the story from all sides. Be sure one of your entries is from the perspective of the God character in the story. How do they compare? Does God really give one group of people the right to slaughter another group and take their land? If not, how do you explain God's presence in the story as depicted in the text? Finally, do you agree with the Grateful Dead's conclusion in "Ramble on Rose" that the grass is indeed *not* always greener on the other side?

(2) In the chapter, the issues of victory and failure in life are raised through the description of the battles to take the promised land. Today's Christianity has seen much that seeks to define success in terms of financial wealth, national pride, winners and losers, and success for some at the expense of others. How do you define success in your life? How do you define failure? Now read the Gospel of Mark in one sitting and answer the two questions again. How did Jesus define success and failure? Does he even use that type of language to interpret life? What is success and power in light of the cruci-

fixion? What "promised lands" have you idealized in your own life that you are willing to destroy other people to get? Was Jesus right . . . is there a way to live in fulfillment of our own dreams and hopes and at the same time equip others to do the same? How has our theology of scarcity and fear of never having enough made a "Jesus way of living" impossible for our species?

(3) Samson and Delilah get a lot of mileage in the songs we discussed in this chapter, from small, one-line references to complete lyrics centered just on their story. Where do you think the staying power of the story comes from? Is it the aspect of betrayal in a romantic relationship that we see played out in our lives all too frequently? Is it because the story has such fascinating characters and the plot has such great twists and turns? If you had to do a character sketch of Delilah listing her good points and bad points, how balanced would it be? Is she all evil and Samson all good? While it is nearly impossible because of the context of the story, try to relate their relationship to some you have had in your life. Can you begin to understand how complicated the issue of betrayal can become? What can you do to begin to forgive yourself and make amends to others you have betrayed? What can you do to begin to forgive others who betrayed you? (NOTE: If you are struggling with this real sense of betrayal, you might try listening alone to Jamie O'Neal's "There Is No Arizona" and using that song of betrayal as a catalyst for letting out the rage and disappointment in your life.)

(4) There has been an extensive treatment of the lyrics of Leonard Cohen's "Hallelujah" in this chapter. It is rich with metaphor and symbolism and captures much of life's complexity as it relates to our connection to the divine and how that plays out in our connection to each other. Get a copy of the lyrics and read them carefully. Try to draw lines between the human condition as expressed by the David story in the song and your own life. Where have you strayed from intimacy with God and others? Can you point to a time in your life when you have begun the difficult processing of returning to the divine presence and to the relationships with people you have hurt or lost along the way? Can you feel the writer's deep sense of integrity as he stands before God with all of his life on display—no secrets, no agendas— with nothing but the "Hallelujah" on his lips? Do you think you could ever be that truly transparent with God and others?

(5) The Jezebel image of a woman has been referenced in some of the songs listed in this chapter. Not the most flattering of images, it is part of the "temptress" image of women that is found throughout various parts of the Bible. How do you think this kind of representation of women throughout Christianity has affected the way women are treated and valued in the world? Is it a valid representation? Does it apply equally to males and females? If so, can you articulate the cultural and religious influences that would have pushed the biblical writers to focus so much of this character issue onto women and not men? Discuss the challenges of the repeated representation of women like Eve, Delilah, and Jezebel in culture and the arts. Does it have an impact over time on the way men view women? What about how women view themselves? What is the male equivalent to this kind of narrow, one-dimensional representation of a group of people?

(6) What other songs can you think of that have references to these biblical stories? What other questions came to mind as you were reading and discussing this section? If there were one concept or thought encountered in this part of the Bible that would cause you to live and be differently than you are now, what would it be and what will you do about it?

Notes

[1] For a thorough description of how this story is constructed and its theological implications, see Mark McEntire, *The Blood of Abel: The Violent Plot in the Hebrew Bible* (Macon GA: Mercer University Press, 1999), 64-74.

[2] For more on these literary dimensions of the book of Judges, see Mark McEntire, *Dangerous Worlds: Living and Dying in Biblical Texts* (Macon GA: Smyth & Helwys, 2004), 37-52.

[3] For a more carefully nuanced readings of the character of Saul, who receives no attention in popular music, see *The Fate of King Saul: An Interpretation of a Biblical Story* (Sheffield: Sheffield University Press, 1980), 23-56; W. Lee Humphreys, *The Tragic Vision and the Hebrew Tradition* (Philadelphia: Fortress Press, 1985), 23-27; and J. Cheryl Exum, *Tragedy and Biblical Narrative: Arrows of the Almighty* (Cambridge: Cambridge University Press, 1992), 17-18.

[4] For more on the complex relationship between David and Saul, see McEntire, *Dangerous Worlds*, 69-82.

[5] The word "hallelujah" is made up of the imperative form of the Hebrew verb meaning "praise" (*hallelu*) and a shortened form of the divine name (*jah*). It appears most frequently in the latter portions of the book of Psalms.

[6] About half of the psalms in the biblical book of Psalms contain David's name in the title, but it is not clear what this means. David may have written them, or they may have been written for or about him. Nevertheless, the tradition of David as a composer has grown until many assume that he wrote all of the psalms in the Bible.

CHAPTER SIX

The Poet's Poets

Singing about Psalms and Wisdom Literature

The Biblical Texts

The middle part of the Old Testament is more difficult to describe succinctly. A number of poetic books appear there that are difficult to classify. By the end of 2 Kings, the Old Testament has told its story, so these books do not participate in the development of a continuous narrative. Some of them are aware of that narrative, and in many ways they are responding to it. This chapter will include songs that refer to the books called Psalms, Job, Ecclesiastes, and the Song of Songs. The books of Job, Proverbs, and Ecclesiastes are often grouped together as the "Wisdom Literature" of the Old Testament, while Psalms and the Song of Songs stand alone as unique books in the canon. Though Job appears first in the common ordering of English Bible, it will be grouped with the remainder of the Wisdom Literature, while Psalms is treated first.

The 150 poems contained in the book of Psalms are songs themselves. Our text of the Bible, however, has left little evidence of how they might have been performed or what they would have sounded like. We are left with little more than the bare words of the poems. Recent research has revealed that the book of Psalms is much more than just a large collection of individual poems, though. It is a carefully crafted literary work that serves a purpose larger than the sum of its 150 parts.[1] Psalm 1 is an appropriate introduction to the book as a whole. It presents competing images of a righteous person and wicked person. Both are described using horticultural imagery. The use of contrasting images and parallel literary structures are both common in the book of Psalms. The righteous person is "like a tree planted beside streams of water." The wicked person, on the other hand, is "chaff which the wind blows away." This contrast presents two ways of life, and the book of Psalms intends to encourage the first way, which will lead to happiness. The tree planted by water thus stands as an entry point to the book of Psalms.[2] It both marks the way for a righteous person and embodies the character of such an individual.

The book of Psalms has long been divided into five books, likely to match the five "Books of Moses" in the Pentateuch. The divisions are 1–41, 42–72, 73–89, 90–106, and 107–150. While the entirety of the book of Psalms has been linked traditionally to David in various ways, David's name appears most frequently in books 1 and 2 in the so-called "titles" found at the beginning of the majority of psalms. These titles appear at the top of about 90 percent of the psalms in the whole book. Approximately half of the titles contain David's name. The titles obviously play a role in the organization of the book, because psalms with similar titles often appear in sequence, but the titles do not fully explain this organization.

Psalms are often classified into groups by type or theme. Psalm 1, along with Psalms 27, 49, 119, and others are classified as wisdom psalms. Some psalms are of mixed type and are difficult to classify.[3] Psalm 23 is the most well-known psalm and perhaps the most well-known passage in the entire Bible. It is sometimes classified as a song of trust or confidence. The most common type of psalm in the first half of the book is the lament. A lament is a complaint to God about one or more difficulties in the life of the singer or singers, including illness, hunger, or persecution by enemies. Psalm 23 plays an important role among these lament psalms. Though outnumbered by laments, such songs of trust keep the reader from forgetting the positive aspects of God's care and protection. Psalm 22 is one of the most severe lament poems in the book. It opens with the line quoted by Jesus from the cross in the Gospels of Mark and Matthew, "My God, my God, why have you forsaken me?" This painful expression of complaint against God is carefully balanced by the soothing words of Psalm 23, yet the more comforting psalm is not blind to the painful realities of life. Standing precisely at its center is the line that the King James Version famously presents as "Yea, though I walk through the valley of the shadow of death . . . ."[4] This line is contained within the shepherd imagery of vv. 1-4 and stands in some contrast to the sudden appearance of the banquet hall celebration of vv. 5-6. The enemies are still present in the final scene, but they are now chained captives, forced to watch the celebration of their defeat. This little poem holds together images of pastoral ease, mortal danger, and raucous celebration in an uneasy tension that befits the first half of the book of Psalms.

Lament psalms tend to follow a pattern that often begins with a cry of despair to God, like that found at the beginning of Psalm 22. This cry is typically followed by specific complaints about the singer's troubles. These might include illness, persecution by enemies, or poverty. After the complaints the singer makes specific requests to God for deliverance. Some form of an expression of confidence that God will deliver usually follows the requests. A final element in a lament often involves some type of promise or vow that the singer will give an offering or other act of praise to God. This pattern creates in a lament poem a general movement from negative to positive emotion. In many ways this polarity of a lament is matched on a larger scale by the book of Psalms itself, which is characterized by a high concentration of lament poems in its first half and a low concentration in the second half. The decreasing concentration of lament psalms is accompanied by a corresponding increase in the more positive types of psalms, like the hymns of praise.[5]

Psalm 57 contains within its title the phrase "Of David . . . when he fled from the presence of Saul in the cave." The psalms that are most intimately connected to the life of David, whether in the titles like Psalm 57 or in traditional understandings and assumptions, are often linked to the period of time when he ran away from the court of Saul and lived the life of a fugitive and a mercenary. These stories are recorded in 1 Samuel 19–30. They are thrilling tales of a bold and daring young man leading a small gang of followers through a variety of dangerous adventures.

The previous chapter explored some of the ways in which David's character is developed, particularly in 1 Samuel. The young king eventually emerges as the Bible's Renaissance man, the great warrior-king-poet. Traditions linking David to the book of Psalms continued to grow for many centuries after his death. Regardless of the historical validity of these developments, the result has been a popular perception, both ancient and modern, that the psalms provide an interior view of the spiritual life of this person. Aside from a few psalms that have no titles, all of the poems in book 1 are exclusively attached to David. This sequence comes to an end after Psalm 41. Psalms 40 and 41, the final psalms in book 1, seem to summarize David's relationship to the God who has made him king over Israel. David has followed a long and difficult path to the throne, but God has delivered him (40:17 and 41:1). The phrase "Happy are those . . ." appears in both of these psalms (40:4 and 41:1) as an echo of the book's beginnings (1:1 and 2:11). After a brief break, psalms attached to David by their titles begin to appear again at 51. Even if David did not write any of the psalms himself, the literary effect of the Old Testament canon is that the reader hears the voice of the character named David reciting these poems.

Psalm 72 brings book 2 to an end and concludes with the enigmatic sentence, "The prayers of David, son of Jesse, have ended."[6] Psalm 73 thus begins book 3 and also initiates a sequence of eleven psalms with the name "Asaph" in the title. Those who understand the book of Psalms to have a plot that reflects the story of Israel associate book 3 with the experience of the exile. Psalm 73 expresses doubts and pains that fit well with such an experience. This psalm has even been labeled "the little Job" because of the sense of suffering it expresses. The opening line, "Surely God is good to the upright, to the pure of heart," seems like a faithful aphorism that will be put to the test in the following lines. The singer's experience does not fit this simplistic statement of faith, and vv. 2-14 express a painful experience, culminating with "I am plagued all day, and punished every morning." The psalm reverses itself in vv. 15-26 when the singer enters the temple and recalls another set of experiences that reflect more positively on God's faithfulness. The final verse of the psalm is a statement of faith that sounds consistent with the one in the first verse, but is much less simplistic. The statement in v. 28 seems less dependent upon the immediate blessings of God.

In the Christian Old Testament, the book of Job comes immediately before Psalms, while in the Jewish Scriptures it comes immediately after. These two books, seemingly so different at first glance, have much in common upon closer examination. We have already noted the connections between Job and Psalm 73. More significantly, both of these books reflect Israel's story of deliverance and prosperity, followed by destruction and exile, followed by restoration.

The book of Job has a distinctive structure. The first two chapters provide a narrative introduction to the story. A heavenly contest is arranged between God and a character called the "adversary" or "accuser."[7] This character accuses Job of only being faithful to God in return for the blessings God provides. To determine whether Job's faith is really only a *quid pro quo* arrangement, God allows the adversary to kill all of Job's children and destroy or take away all of his possessions. Job's faith appears to be intact at the end of these personal disasters, so the adversary asks to be able to attack Job's own body. God gives permission again, requiring only that Job not be killed. The narrative ends with a destitute Job, riddled by a skin disease, sitting in the dust as his three friends arrive to visit him. Beginning in chapter 3, the book of Job becomes a long sequence of poetic speeches. For a long time, these speeches are carefully ordered. Job speaks, then the three friends—Eliphaz, Bildad, and Zophar—speak in turn, each followed by a response from Job. As this cycle of speeches nears the end of its third repetition, the third speech of Zophar suddenly turns up missing. This is the last we hear from these three characters. For the most part, they have attacked Job and have argued that all of his suffering must be the result of some sin he has committed. He should repent and ask God's forgiveness. Job steadfastly refuses to accept blame for his predicament. He insists on his innocence, of which the narrative had also assured the reader in 1:1 and 1:8. The poetic dialogue continues at this point, but other voices enter the conversation, including that of God. The book of Job begins moving toward a conclusion as Job experiences the divine encounter he has longed for ever since his affliction began. God speaks to Job and he is satisfied, but the poetic portion of the book offers no resolution to Job's difficulties. The narrative framework resumes at 42:7. Here God reaffirms Job's righteousness, castigates the friends for their false speech, and restores Job's life. The ultimate concern of the book of Job is how we talk about God in the midst of suffering.[8] The "friends" blame the victim, while Job, the victim, demands and receives a divine encounter. The quest for this encounter does not resolve the problem of suffering, but it keeps Job's life pointed in the right direction.

The book of Ecclesiastes is another component of the Wisdom Literature that has much in common with Job. The easy equations of righteousness and success, which often characterize the book of Proverbs and which are mouthed by Job's companions, are also called into question in this book. Ecclesiastes seems to be a rather disjointed tour of the life and thought of someone called *Qoheleth*, which could mean the Teacher, the Preacher, or the Gatherer. The montage of images is tied together, however, by several recurring lines. Among them are "vanity of vanities, all is vanity," "all this is vanity and a chasing after wind," "there is nothing new under the sun," and "eat, drink, and find enjoyment." The most well-known passage in the book is 3:1-8, the rhythmic little poem introduced by the line "For everything there is a season." The remainder of the poem is a list of opposites, everything from kill and heal to weep and laugh to war and peace. The poem claims there is a time for each of these. It is difficult to know how to understand such a claim. For many readers it is tempting to see this as a confirmation of some kind of grand, divine plan for the world. Within the context of the general sense of futility in Ecclesiastes, however, it looks more like a fatalistic acceptance of the oppositional nature of the world. For modern readers, the issue may be whether we can have any effect on the nature of these matters and their seasons. The book of Ecclesiastes goes on after this poem, noting some positive aspects of life, like friendship and contentment, but the overall tone still protests against claims of order, fairness, and justice in the world. The encouragement to "eat, drink, and find enjoyment" (2:24, 3:13, 5:18, etc.) promotes an attitude of contentment, but it is also a resignation that there may not be much more sense to life than this.

Ecclesiastes 12:9-13, the final five verses of the book, raise serious questions. The "Teacher" is introduced in 1:1, and then his voice speaks from 1:2 to 12:8. The final five verses, often called the epilogue of the book, are spoken by the voice of a narrator and refer to the Teacher in third person. More significantly, this epilogue espouses a more traditional theology, including fear of God and obedience to God's commandments, that stands in some tension to the questions raised by the rest of the book. The epilogue serves to end the book on a more positive note, but the notion that it has been added on simply to silence an important voice of dissent or protest causes some readers to be suspicious of its simplistic piety.

The book commonly known as the Song of Solomon, more properly the Song of Songs, is difficult to fit into any category because it is so different from anything else in the Bible. It appears to be a collection of love poems that tell the story of a series of encounters between two lovers. Discomfort with such subject matter has produced a long history of elaborate interpretive strategies related to this book. Within Judaism and Christianity the book has been read as an allegory of the relationship between God and Israel or Christ and the church. Such readings may be interesting and useful, but it must be admitted that they impose a framework that is not within the text itself. The most straightforward reading is still that which understands the book as romantic poetry. The Song of Songs may be understood according to the following outline:

1:2–2:7	A first meeting between the lovers
2:8–3:5	The lovers attempt to be together despite obstacles
3:6–4:5	The wedding festivities
4:6–5:16	The sexual encounter between the lovers
6:1–7:6	The lovers assume a royal identity
7:7–8:4	The lovers sing about being together
8:5-14	A final romantic encounter[9]

One conclusion that may be derived from a careful reading of this book as a whole is that romantic love is an aspect of life that the Bible takes seriously. Still, interpretations of the book frequently extract portions of it and attempt to spiritualize them.

Songs about Psalms, Wisdom, and Romance

Bob Marley survived an assassination attempt in 1976, and his 1980 song "Forever Loving Jah" seems to be, in part, a response to this experience. As in many other songs, Marley uses the abbreviated name for God, Jah, commonly used in the psalms and in his own Rastafarian religious tradition. This song is about encountering opposition. Marley had become the musical voice of the poor in Jamaica, but this brought political opposition including the assassination attempt. The final verse of the song contains a quotation of Psalm 1:3. In the face of the opposition and oppression experienced by Marley and his followers, he encourages himself and his listeners to be like the "tree planted by the river of water," the image used in Psalm 1 to portray a righteous person. Psalm 1 equates righteousness with delighting in God's law and contends that a person who does so will be happy. For Marley, the equivalent is "loving Jah." This is both the river that sustains him and the fruit brought forth "in due season." The previous verse of the song points in opposition to the "fool" in a way similar to that in which Psalm 1 speaks of a wicked person, but the direct reference here to "what has been hidden from the wise and the prudent" being "revealed to the babe and the suckling" comes from Luke 10:21. This is the one place where Marley's reference to Psalm 1 creates some tension between the positive attitude to wisdom in the psalms and a mistrust of wisdom in other places.

The hip-hop hit "Gangsta's Paradise," by the artist known as Coolio, opens with a quotation of Psalm 23:4a. This song itself is a long, detailed lament over the pains and difficulties of living in a neighborhood ruled by gangs and crime.[10] So, the line from Psalm 23 fits within it much like the psalm itself fits into its surroundings in the book of Psalms. The singer of "Gangsta's Paradise" is a participant in this life of violence and death, but manages to see beyond it. Thus, the frequently repeated lines, "Tell me why are we so blind to see, that the ones we hurt are you and me." As mentioned earlier in this chapter, many of the poems in the first half of the book of Psalms have been attached by tradition to the fugitive days of David, a set of stories that can easily be compared to the life of a bandit or gangster. So, any initial impulse to reject connections between Psalm 23 and a violent gang life need to be carefully considered. The exposure to death that the quotation of Psalm 23:4a highlights at the beginning of the song causes the singer to evaluate his life. He seems to want to escape this way of living, but is not sure whether it is possible. The immanence of death reappears in the middle of the song. The line "I'm twenty-three now, but will I live to see twenty-four?" can hardly be accidental in its choice of numbers. Psalm 24 is a hymn of praise to God, as creator and king, abiding in his holy temple. "The ones who have clean hands and pure hearts" (24:4) will join God there. Will the singer in "Gangsta's Paradise" ever arrive in such a place?

Of course, composers have set many of the poems in Psalms to music throughout the centuries and in modern times. This is not the same thing as using elements from the Old Testament in a song, though, so such songs do not easily fit into the scope of this book. One example that is on the border between these two types of musical composition using the Bible is the U2 song called simply "Forty." The components of the song are a combination of close quotation and paraphrase of Psalm 40:1-3. The repeated lines of the chorus are based on the first line of v. 3., "He put a new song in my mouth." The plaintive cry in "Forty," "How long to sing this song," however, does not appear in Psalm 40. The "How long . . ." cry is a frequent element of lament psalms like Psalm 13. This line in "Forty" links it to another U2 song, "Two Hearts Beat as One," which was on the same album and was released with it as a single. The frequently repeated "How long, how long must we sing this song" in "Two Hearts Beat as One" also draws on the lament tradition of the biblical psalms. Like a lament psalm, and like the book of Psalms itself, "Forty" seems to move back and forth between the positive and negative poles of religious experience.

A little more than halfway through Lauryn Hill's powerful, hip-hop "thesis," "Final Hour," the line "And I remain calm reading the 73rd Psalm," appears. When Hill received the Grammy Award for her album *The Miseducation of Lauryn Hill,* she carried a Bible with her to the podium and read from Psalm 73. There are earlier biblical references in the song, including the names Simeon, Israel, and Moses and Aaron. The song as a whole seems to be an indictment of money and power. While this indictment may be aimed in part at hip-hop culture, lines like "Make a slum lord be the tenant" provide it with a much larger scope. Psalm 73 expresses a great deal of frustration at its beginning. The writer is uncertain about two ideas often central to Israelite religion—that wisdom and righteousness lead to prosperity and that foolishness and wickedness bring destruction. Like Psalm 73, "Final Hour" acknowledges that its immediate situation is one in which the wicked prosper, but it holds out hope that a reversal is coming. Reading Psalm 73 thus provides the singer with a sense of calm in a difficult situation. The recurring refrain warns of this reversal, urging the listener to resist the temptations of money and power and ". . . keep your eyes on the final hour."

Joni Mitchell's "Sire of Sorrows" is explicitly about the character named Job, and the song reflects the structure of the book. Most significantly, multiple voices appear in the song, representing the characters who speak in the book. The opening lines take the listener directly into Job's condition. The reference to "festering flesh" locates Job in the part of the story at the end of Job 2 where he has lost everything and is ill. The words of Job in the song quickly turn to questions directed toward God, the kinds of questions found in abundance in Job 3–4. The first two verses of the song illustrate the stark differences between Job's former life of blessing and success and his current plight. The striking final line of the second verse, "you make everything I dread and everything I fear come true," is a close match with Job 3:25, but the slight changes in grammar may cause us to miss the implication. When Job says, "The thing that I fear has overcome me," this is most easily understood as a reference to 1:1, where the thing Job fears is God. The voice of Job's "friends" shows up in the background vocal "Man is the sire of sorrow." Just as in the book, the other voices in the song blame Job for his difficulties. "Sire of Sorrow" comes to an end without a resolution. Job is still asking his questions, such as "What have I done to you?" The other voices in the song still make their accusations: "Oh your guilt must weigh so greatly."

The hit song from the 1970s called "Dust in the Wind," written by Kerry Livgren and made popular by the band Kansas, shares much common language and many common images with the book of Ecclesiastes. Ecclesiastes 3:20 echoes the famous lines in Genesis 3:19, and both feed into the sense of futility expressed in "Dust in the Wind." Repeated images of dust, water, wind, and death serve to emphasize this sense of futility in both the song and the text. Ecclesiastes 1:7 contains the classic, poetic line "All rivers run to the sea, but the sea is never full." The sense of smallness and emptiness is also expressed by the phrase "Just a drop of water in and endless sea" in "Dust in the Wind." The futility of life expressed by this song may serve to point to the epilogue in Ecclesiastes 12:9-13. Many human beings are uncomfortable with the possibility that life does not have an obvious meaning and purpose. A sense of futility dominates the book of Ecclesiastes, but the epilogue punctuates the book with a fairly standard exhortation to obey God. "Dust in the Wind" does not have an ending that contains and controls its sense of uncertainty. Instead, the song slowly fades away with its desperate claim, "Everything is dust in the wind," repeated over and over again.

A band called Sixpence None the Richer, which took its name from a story told by C. S. Lewis in his chapter on faith in *Mere Christianity*, borrowed significantly from Ecclesiastes in their song "Meaningless." This word is a reasonable translation of the Hebrew word *hebel*, which is commonly translated as "vanity." The first verse of the song, like the first chapter of Ecclesiastes, uses numerous images from nature to demonstrate the cyclical futility of life. The chorus then claims that life has no purpose. In the face of this lack of purpose, the second verse, again like the book of Ecclesiastes, advises the simple enjoyment of life's pleasures, such as food and drink. Along with words that echo the famous "Eat, drink, and be merry" of Ecclesiastes 8:15, the song also adds the familiar line "Gather ye rosebuds while ye may," from the seventeenth-century English poet Robert Herrick. Between the end of the second verse and the final repetition of the chorus, the line "fear your God this is all I know" intrudes. This line is a close match to Ecclesiastes 12:13. What makes the song and text significantly different here is the placement of this pious sentiment. In Ecclesiastes this is the final thought, and it helps contain the expressions of futility that fill the book. In the song, the final occurrence of the refrain causes the song to end with the line "Now I don't have a reason to live anymore." The sense of meaninglessness from which the song gets its name is uncontained.

The most well-known song that makes use of Ecclesiastes is Pete Seeger's classic "Turn, Turn, Turn." The song was made famous by the popular recording of the Byrds during the height of the Vietnam era. Its popularity was revived in the 1990s when the song appeared on the soundtrack of the movie *Forrest Gump.* The song comes close simply to reproducing the biblical text from Ecclesiastes. The repeated chorus of the song is close to 3:1, except for the exhortation "turn, turn, turn." The paired elements in the song are taken from the text. Each pair has what might be interpreted as a positive and a negative element. Of fourteen pairs in Ecclesiastes 3:2-8, six have the positive element first and eight have the negative element first. The song has twelve of the pairs, with eight of these placing the positive element first. These changes may be done to enhance the rhythmic quality of the song, but the result is a slight realignment of the poem to place the positive elements in the first position more often. The major change in the song comes only at the end, when its purpose to promote peace becomes clear. This move by the songwriter raises an important issue that is also present in the Ecclesiastes text. It is easy to read Ecclesiastes 3:1-8 in a fatalistic manner. Good and bad times come and go and human beings should simply accept this rhythmic quality of life. Given the overall context of the book of Ecclesiastes, such a fatalistic interpretation is difficult to deny. This does not fit well with the current attitude in Western culture that we can solve at least some of life's problems. The central issue in the song becomes war, and since wars are started by human choices they ought to be able to be stopped by human choices. Thus the song concludes, "A time for peace, I swear it's not too late."

A song called "Tripping Billies" by the Dave Matthews Band makes repeated use of the line "Eat, drink, and be merry, for tomorrow we die." This is an obvious reference to a similar repeated refrain in the book of Ecclesiastes.[11] It is also combined with a saying in Isaiah 22:13, "Let us eat and drink, for tomorrow we die." This Isaiah text is actually a condemnation of such a festive attitude because God had "called to weeping and mourning." The Isaiah reference and its context will be discussed further in the next chapter. In Ecclesiastes, this saying takes several forms, and of course it appears differently in various translations. The closest to the saying in the song is the King James Version of 8:15. The meaning of this song is difficult to determine. It does appear to be a reference to drug use and a carefree lifestyle. The singer seems to be enjoying a happy and carefree experience with friends. The possibility that mind-altering drugs are involved is problematic, but should not completely obscure an important issue raised by the song and the frequent acknowledgment of the role of pleasure in life by the

"Teacher" in the book of Ecclesiastes. Amid the perplexities and contradictions of life, what role ought enjoyment, satisfaction, or contentment play for people of faith? Certain segments of the Christian church tend to advocate, either directly or indirectly, a sense of detachment from the physical world. The question asked in "Tripping Billies"—"Why would you care to get out of this place?"—helps to highlight this issue. The speaker in Ecclesiastes urges an enjoyment of pleasure that is connected to the rest of life.[12] A holistic understanding of creation makes a life that detaches the spiritual from the physical appear unhealthy and inconsistent.

A song called "Banner Year," performed by the band Five Iron Frenzy, contains an enigmatic quotation of Song of Songs 2:4. In this biblical text, the female character is speaking of her lover, and in the King James Version, she says, "He brought me to the banqueting house, and his banner over me was love." Near the end of "Banner Year," the sentence "His banner over me was love" appears. The song identifies two years, 1864 and 1868, as "banner years." Both years refer to massacres of Native Americans in the American West. The first part of the song refers to the 1864 massacre at Sand Creek. The first references to "flag" and "banner" appear here. The Cheyenne chief, Black Kettle, was promised in a treaty that if he flew an American flag his people would not be attacked. This promise was ignored, however, and Black Kettle's people were slaughtered. Four years later, in a similar incident, Black Kettle and the others living with him in an Oklahoma settlement were massacred despite the white flag flying above their village that was supposed to protect them.[13] The sentence from Song of Songs 2:4 is obviously taken out of context here, but is employed with great irony by the songwriter. The phrase may be familiar because of its use in a popular children's gospel chorus. Thus, most people who recognize it are already unaware of its romantic context in the Song of Songs. Instead, this popular usage of the phrase goes along with the common spiritual allegory approach to interpreting the Song of Songs. The final lines of "Banner Year" memorialize the tragic life of Black Kettle: "No flag flies, no banner waves, see the empty pole above his empty grave." The banner that should signify love in the form of life and protection instead flies over death.

Kate Bush's album *Red Shoes* contains a song called "The Song of Solomon." The meaning of this song is not entirely clear, but it seems to be expressing dissatisfaction with the kind of romantic language that fills the book called the Song of Songs. The first verse argues that the "Song of Solomon" is the song of those who are lonely. Instead of words, the woman singing the refrain asks, "Write me your poetry in motion." The second verse quotes a number of phrases from Song of Songs 2:5-6. Again, the refrain follows and seems to accuse these words of being "excuses" and "bullshit." The third verse uses two floral images from the Song of Songs—"the Rose of Sharon" and the "Lily of the Valley" (2:1). The final occurrence of the refrain or a fragment of it implies that such words are a useless substitute for real sexuality. This song raises interesting issues about the nature of the Song of Songs, its purpose in the Bible, and appropriate understandings of sexuality for people of faith. Does the Song of Songs represent authentic language of love, or is it manipulative and self-centered?

Summary and Questions for Reflection

The books commonly called the "poetic books" of the Old Testament form a rich and diverse literary collection. These books arose out of the context of ancient Israel and the collective experience of its people. We know little about how these biblical poems, songs, and proverbs were actually used within Israelite culture. It is easy to imagine them playing a similar role to that of music in our own culture. They express the emotion of the artists who produce them and touch similar feelings within those who hear and read them. Here are some questions to help you explore many of the issues raised in the songs and related biblical texts discussed above.

(1) Consider the dualism of the wicked and the righteous person presented by the Psalms and the characteristics and images that accompany both. Is that the way you have found your world to be? Is it too simple and concrete? What parts of yourself can you identify that represent each character—both a tree planted by the water and the chaff the wind blows away? If life and the people in it are really more complicated than the dualism above suggests, how do we lean into the righteous person we say we want to be? What disciplines and life practices could you change that would lead you toward the tree planted by the water in Psalm 1? How many songs, poems, lines from literature, etc., can you name that have that line in it? Why do you think this imagery is so strong in the human psyche?

(2) The psalms (and the songs that reference them in this book) are rich with the balance of suffering and trust in God that is inherent in the human condition. Jesus' use of a psalm as a means of expressing his suffering and needs on the cross speak volumes of what they represent in the way of a functional

spiritual purpose in life. So consider that classic lament psalm form: cry, complaint, request for deliverance, expression of confidence in God, and promise of praise to God for God's deliverance. Would you be willing to write your own lament psalm to express a deep sense of hurt in your life? Would you be willing to share it with a friend or perhaps work with a musician you know to put it to music? Would you sing/pray the psalm every day until your suffering has passed as a helpful way of dealing with your fears and frustrations?

(3) The book of Job is the ultimate expression of the human confusion that accompanies suffering we haven't earned and don't deserve. We all struggle with the sense that life is not fair . . . and for good reason. It is not. We are all subject to suffering from natural disasters, being deceived, being blamed for something we did not do, and enduring illnesses we did nothing to cause and cannot prevent. What do we do with this reality in life as children of a loving and compassionate God? Do the songs we have mentioned about Job do justice to the complexity and severity of the issue? Pick one to which you relate well; listen to the song and read the lyrics several times. Does that process help you look to the heavens and cry out "why?" Do you feel better or worse when you are finished?

(4) The poem in Ecclesiastes 3:1-8, "For everything there is a season . . . ," has surfaced in many songs and various forms of the arts throughout the years. Perhaps some of its great power lies in viewing each line as a continuum. It is not so much that there is a time for being born and a time to die, but that every moment of our life we are being born and we are dying. We have not truly been born until we come to grips with our ultimate fate, for the moment we are born we have begun to die. Looking at the words of the passage in this light, does it give you more hope for the future or less? How does it make you feel to consider that every sowing is also a reaping, everything accomplished is a beginning to something else? Does it help you get a better sense of the cycles of life? If so, how? Can you describe a time in your life when an ending was a beginning or the other way around?

(5) You cannot read far into the Old Testament before you are confronted with issues of social justice and equality. Many of the songs we referenced in this chapter allude to the inherent inequities of the world and the effect they have on the poor and the oppressed. Did any song in particular ring true to

you on this theme? Do you share the artist's concern that the inequities of our financial and social systems are real and have dire consequences? What about their assertions that a better day is coming? Is it coming from God? From us? From both? What does the Jesus story of suffering and redemption have to do with our leaving the world better than we found it?

(6) What other songs can you think of that have references to these biblical stories? What other questions came to mind as you were reading and discussing this section? If there were one concept or thought encountered in this part of the Bible that would cause you to live and be differently than you are now, what would it be and what will you do about it?

Notes

[1] See the description of how the book of Psalms functions as a book in John H. Tullock and Mark McEntire, *The Old Testament Story*, 7th ed. (Upper Saddle River NJ: Prentice Hall, 2004), 350-51.

[2] For a full development of this idea, see William P. Brown, *Seeing the Psalms: A Theology of Metaphor* (Louisville: Westminster John Knox, 2004), 55-79.

[3] For a complete list of psalms by type, see Bernhard W. Anderson, *Out of the Depths: The Psalms Speak for Us Today* (Philadelphia: Westminster Press, 1983), 239-42.

[4] More recent English translations have, probably correctly, abandoned this phrase for something like, "Even though I walk through the darkest valley" (NRSV). This change, and the exchange of the King James Version's final word "forever," for something like "all of my life" distances the more modern English translations from the Christian ideas of death, resurrection, and eternal life that so aided its explosion in popularity over the last century. For a thorough discussion of such developments, see William L. Holladay, *The Psalms Through Three Thousand Years: Prayerbook of a Cloud of Witnesses* (Minneapolis: Fortress Press, 1993), 359-71.

[5] For much more on this kind of deliberate shaping of the book of Psalms, see Nancy L. deClaisse-Walford, *Reading from the Beginning: The Shaping of the Hebrew Psalter* (Macon GA: Mercer University Press, 1997) and J. Clinton McCann, *Shape and Shaping of the Psalter* (Sheffield: Sheffield Academic Press, 1993).

[6] This line is puzzling for a number of reasons. First, Psalm 72 contains the name of Solomon, not David, in its title. Second, many of the psalms in book 2 have names other than David in their titles. Third, many psalms after 72 have David in their titles.

[7] The Hebrew word for "adversary" is *satan*, a word that later became the basis for the name of the character called Satan. Some English translations carry this development back into the text of the book of Job and call this character Satan.

[8] For a well-developed presentation of this understanding, see Gustavo Gutierrez, *On Job: God Talk and the Suffering of the Innocent* (Maryknoll NY: Orbis, 1984).

[9] See the further discussion of this structure of the book in Tullock and McEntire, *The Old Testament Story*, 347.

[10] See the discussion of this song and an accompanying lesson plan in Mark Roncace, "Psalm 23 and Modern Worldviews," in *Teaching the Bible: Practical Strategies for Classroom Discussion*, ed. Mark Roncace and Patrick Gray (Atlanta: Society of Biblical Literature, 2005), 205-206.

[11] See the discussion of this song in Mark Roncace, "The Structure of Ecclesiastes and the Views of the Teacher," in *Teaching the Bible*, 232-33.

[12] For an eloquent discussion of this important issue and the need to make our religious speech match the way we actually live, see Wendell Berry, *Jayber Crow* (New York: Counterpoint, 2000), 160-61.

[13] The stories of Black Kettle and the Cheyenne people played a significant role in the recent television miniseries *Into the West* on the TNT Network.

CHAPTER SEVEN

Shouting in the Wind

Singing about the Prophets

The Biblical Texts

The prophetic literature of the Old Testament consists of four large collections or scrolls. The first three each carry the name of a single prophetic figure—Isaiah, Jeremiah, and Ezekiel. The fourth collection, the Book of the Twelve, has more often been treated as twelve separate, small prophetic books, beginning with Hosea and ending with Malachi. These scrolls are large and complex literary works that contain a dizzying variety of materials and assume familiarity with many of the traditions of ancient Israel. Because it is so difficult to grasp and engage a full prophetic scroll and its purpose, the most common use of these books within Christian tradition has been to extract small pieces out of context in order to support preconceived theological positions. Only in the last few decades has significant attention been paid to these scrolls as holistic literary works.

All four of the prophetic scrolls in the Old Testament share common background. This background may be understood in terms of the three major crises confronted by Israel in the eighth through fifth centuries BCE.

The first of these crises was brought on by the expansion of the Assyrian Empire in the second half of the eighth century. As this empire, centered in Mesopotamia, expanded westward, the small nations of the ancient Near East, including Israel and Judah, were threatened with destruction. This threat was realized for the northern nation of Israel in the year 722 BCE when it was overrun and its population dispersed. The southern nation of Judah was not conquered at this time but was exposed to significant threat by the looming Assyrian Empire that had reached its northern border. Much of the first half of the book of Isaiah, along with the portions of the Book of the Twelve known as Hosea, Amos, Micah, Jonah, and Nahum seem to be prophetic responses to this crisis.

As the Assyrian Empire declined throughout the seventh century, the Babylonian Empire, also centered in Mesopotamia, grew in power. By the last quarter of the seventh century, Babylon was the dominant political and military power in the ancient Near East. The Babylonian Empire also expanded westward toward the territory of the other great empire of that time, Egypt. Judah was caught in between these two empires, with the Babylonians encroaching upon its territory as the seventh century came to an end. During the last decade of the seventh century and first decade of the sixth century, a series of invasions and deportations by the Babylonians weakened Judah's status as an independent nation. This threat culminated in the destruction of the city of Jerusalem and the deportation of many of the leading citizens of Judah in 586 BCE. At this point, the Judean monarchy came to an end, and Israel entered the period of its history commonly known as "the exile." This Babylonian crisis forms the primary background for most of Isaiah 40–55, almost all of the book of Jeremiah, Ezekiel 1–39, and the portions of the Book of the Twelve known as Zephaniah and Habakkuk.

The third and final crisis is somewhat more difficult to define because it does not involve invasion and conquest by a foreign empire. This crisis is sometimes called the "restoration crisis." The period known as the restoration began when Judahites who had been exiled to Babylon began to return to Jerusalem to attempt to rebuild it and the nation of Judah. This process began when the Persian Empire, led by King Cyrus, defeated the Babylonians and began releasing many of its captive peoples to return to their homelands. The Decree of Cyrus, releasing the citizens of Judah, is commonly dated to 538 BCE. The attempt to restore the nation of Judah, the city of Jerusalem, and the temple became a crisis because it was a difficult process that met with mixed results. Many citizens of Judah had stayed behind and constructed new ways of life in the damaged land. These people and the ones returning from Babylon did not reunite easily. The restored community managed to rebuild the temple in about two decades and a walled city of Jerusalem in about a century, but they apparently never freed themselves from Persian political control and did not reestablish the monarchy. Moreover, the restored community struggled economically for many years.[1] The new community struggled with competing political and religious structures, creating another crisis period within its history. Isaiah 56–66, Ezekiel 40–48, and the parts of the Book of the Twelve known as Haggai, Zechariah, and Malachi address this period from a prophetic perspective.

As the discussion above indicates, the book of Isaiah is a long, complex literary work compiled over a period of two to three centuries. It contains prophetic responses to a wide variety of religious and political situations, which are addressed using a variety of literary forms. The most common literary form is the prophetic oracle, a unit of speech attributed to a prophetic voice. The two most common types of oracles are judgment oracles and salvation oracles, in which the prophet mediates "the word of the LORD" to the people. The book of Isaiah has a general sense of narrative movement from negative to positive because judgment oracles dominate the first half of the book, while salvation oracles dominate the second half. The character named Isaiah appears only occasionally in the book in chapters 6–8, 20, and 36–39. It is not clear to what extent the reader is to assume that he is the voice speaking in the other parts of the book. The disappearance of this character after chapter 39, and his complete absence from the second half of the book, causes many readers to see a significant shift in the book's purpose and intent at chapter 40. This coincides with the shift from a perspective located primarily in the period of the Assyrian crisis to a perspective associated with the Babylonian crisis.[2]

One important component of the first half of the book of Isaiah is the collection of "Oracles against the Nations" in Isaiah 13–23. While the opening chapters of the book focus on God's judgment of Israel, this collection turns the attention of God's wrath on the other nations of the ancient Near East. Amid oracles against Babylon, Egypt, Tyre, Moab, and Damascus, Isaiah 21:1-10 is designated as an "oracle concerning the wilderness of the sea." This oracle becomes more specific in v. 9 when it mentions the fall of Babylon. The role of a prophet is developed in this poem as the speaker says in v. 8, "Upon a watchtower I stand, O LORD." The prophet is called to be an observer and to proclaim what he sees. Ambiguity arises in this section, however, as the Isaiah character recedes into the background. Other than one brief story in Isaiah 20, he is not visible in Isaiah 13–35. To whom are we to imagine these oracles against the nations are being declared? Are they warnings for the likes of Babylon and Egypt, or are they words of reassurance for Israel concerning the destruction of its enemies?

The book of Jeremiah is much more biographical than the book of Isaiah. In many ways the prophetic career of the character named Jeremiah functions as a framework for the book. The general movement of the book of Jeremiah from a primarily negative tone centered upon messages of destruction in its first half to a more positive expression of salvation in its second half is even more pronounced than in the book of Isaiah. Jeremiah 1:10 introduces six verbs with the saying "to pluck up and pull down, to destroy and overthrow, to build and plant." Combinations of these verbs appear at prominent places elsewhere in the book such as 24:6, 29:28, 31:28, and 42:10, where they play an important role in developing themes of destruction and salvation. The unique feature that most distinguishes the book of Jeremiah from the other prophetic books is a series of lament poems, often called the "complaints" or "confessions" of Jeremiah. These poems are spread throughout chapters 11–20 and have earned Jeremiah the nickname "the Weeping Prophet." Such a characterization is also present in famous paintings of Jeremiah by Rembrandt and Michelangelo. Like no other prophet in the Old Testament, Jeremiah struggles with the inner turmoil and personal loss that come with his role.

The book of Ezekiel begins with the account of the prophet's initial call, so, in a way similar to the book of Jeremiah, the prophetic career of Ezekiel acts as something of a framework for the book. Perhaps a more significant framing device is the series of four visions spread through the book. The vision that accompanies the call experience in Ezekiel 1–2 is the first of these four. The second vision, in Ezekiel 8–11, portrays the presence or "glory" of God as it departs from the temple in Jerusalem, preparing for the destruction of the temple by the invading Babylonian army. The third vision in Ezekiel 37 is the most famous of the four. In it the prophet is transported in an ecstatic experience to a valley full of skeletons. These skeletons turn out to be those of the slain army of the Israelites remaining from their defeat by the Babylonians. As Ezekiel watches, these skeletons are reanimated and recovered with flesh, and the vision ends with this reconstituted army standing upright. This vision has captured imaginations throughout Christian history to such a degree that the phrase "valley of the dry bones" is commonly recognized in cultures in which the Bible has a significant place. The fourth vision, in Ezekiel 40–48, is a long and detailed description of a new temple to replace the one destroyed by the Babylonians. This final vision plays on the earlier ones, reversing God's departure in Ezekiel 8–11 and utilizing the power of restoration found in Ezekiel 37.

The Book of the Twelve is a complex prophetic scroll that is difficult to describe succinctly. Each of the twelve components has an individual identity, yet forms part of the whole.[3] The historical contexts this collection addresses extend from the Assyrian crisis of the eighth century down to the struggles of the restoration period in the fifth century. The Book of the Twelve opens with Hosea, a prophetic work that appears to address a situation during which both Israel and Judah are threatened by an advancing Assyrian Empire from the north. A distinctive feature of the book of Hosea is a set of brief narratives in which the prophet named Hosea acts as a character. Most of the components of the Book of the Twelve do not have this feature.[4] The most prominent narrative feature in the book of Hosea is the description of the prophet's marriage(s) in Hosea 1 and 3. In 1:2, Hosea is commanded to "Take for yourself a wife of harlotry and children of harlotry." The next verse then reports that Hosea marries Gomer, daughter of Diblayim, and has a son with her. The birth of the son is followed by the birth of the daughter and then another son. Each of the three children is given a symbolic name representing an aspect of the broken relationship between God and Israel. The remainder of Hosea 1 and all of Hosea 2 are filled with prophetic oracles, after which the story of Hosea continues. In 3:1 the LORD tells Hosea to "Go, love a woman, a lover of a companion and an adulteress." In this case, the woman's name is never provided, so it is uncertain whether this is still Gomer or someone else. No children from this union are mentioned in the text.

The remainder of the book of Hosea consists of prophetic oracles that seem to be related to the time of the divided monarchy in the Assyrian period. Some of these oracles develop the theme of Israel as God's unfaithful wife, so Hosea's marriage to Gomer serves as a symbolic act demonstrating Israel's adulterous idolatry.[5] The words of judgment in the book are primarily reserved for the nation of Israel, but God seems torn between the desire to punish and the compassion God has for Israel, which is depicted as God's child, especially in Hosea 11. So, while the book of Hosea begins with the metaphor of God as husband and Israel as unfaithful wife, it moves to the metaphor of God as parent and Israel as disobedient child.

Like other prophetic books, the book of Hosea is filled with many voices. The punctuation of the Hebrew text does not always make clear who is speaking and where their speech begins and ends. Hosea 9:7 is an example of a verse that is potentially confusing because of this feature. Many English translations use additional punctuation, including quotation marks, to try to clarify the situation. Thus, the New Revised Standard Version views this verse in three parts. The first part introduces a quotation by Israel, the second part is the quotation itself, and the third part is a response to the quotation, perhaps by the prophet. It is essential to remember the dialogical nature of prophetic books, especially when small parts are being pulled out and placed in other contexts.

The book of Amos is in the third position in the Book of the Twelve. It is often associated with Hosea because the two books come from about the same period and address the Assyrian crisis. The book of Amos consists almost entirely of oracular material, with little narrative content aside from the intriguing story of Amos and a rival prophet named Amaziah in Amos 7. Because it opens with a series of "oracles against the nations," the book has an international focus, but these oracles lead into pronouncements against Judah and Israel. The primary theme of Amos is the injustice being practiced in Israel and the threat of God's judgment on that injustice. Amos's concern for justice centers upon issues of economics, violence, and oppression. While Amos is perhaps the book most often connected to the cause of justice, this is a concern reflected in the other components of the Book of the Twelve around it, like Joel and Micah. Both of these books contain echoes of a familiar phrase found first in Isaiah 2:4b, "They shall beat their swords to plowshares and their spears to pruning hooks." Joel, the second part of the Book of the Twelve, reverses both parts of this phrase in 3:10 and converts the pronouns to second person. It is, therefore, a call to war, a proclamation to the nations that they should prepare to be attacked by Israel's God. Micah 4:3, on the other hand, repeats the phrase exactly as it is found in Isaiah. The prominent, multiple uses of this saying make it an ideal image of war and peace, an issue central to many components of the Book of the Twelve.

The book of Jonah stands out in the Book of the Twelve as something unique. While Jonah is clearly a prophet, this is a short story about him rather than a collection of his prophetic sayings. Issues concerning the historicity of the book of Jonah often obscure the book's important ideas. The book has many bizarre elements, including the use of dice to determine the cause of a storm, a man living in the belly of a fish for three days then getting spit out alive, the cows of Nineveh repenting after Jonah's preaching, a plant growing large enough to shade Jonah in one day, and a worm destroying that same plant in a day. Whether one accepts the story with these elements as a literal account of a historical event or not, the satirical tone should not be lost. Jonah, an Israelite prophet, is commanded to go and preach to the people of Nineveh, a despised enemy. Jonah evades this call because he believes God will forgive the Ninevites rather than punishing them. Once the events involving the storm and the fish persuade Jonah to go to Nineveh, his worst fears are realized. They repent and God spares them. Jonah goes out into the desert to pout, and the events involving the plant and the worm take place there. The book of Jonah is not about whether a man can live inside a fish, but about whether enemies can repent and be forgiven. It is not about what kind of plant can grow this fast, but about how we will respond to God's compassion for others. Jonah is a caricature of a prophet who preaches gloom and doom and hopes it happens.

It is difficult to assign the book of Daniel a place in the Christian canon. The Hebrew canon places Daniel in the third section, the Writings, rather than in the second section, the Prophets. The first half of the book, a series of tales about young Hebrews living within the Babylonian Empire, has strong affinities with the book of Esther and the book of Tobit within the Apocrypha. Like the book of Esther, there is a Greek version of the book of Daniel that has significant additional material not present in the Hebrew version of the book.[6] These extra parts of Daniel are included within the material called the Apocrypha, which is placed after the Old Testament in some Protestant Christian Bibles. The second half of the book of Daniel is composed of several apocalyptic visions. The material most similar to this in the remainder of the Old Testament is the series of visions presented in the last several chapters of Zechariah. In the Christian Old Testament, the book of Daniel sits rather uneasily between Ezekiel and Hosea, the first book in the Book of the Twelve. The character named Daniel is not presented as a prophet. His role as an interpreter of dreams and, eventually, an advisor to a foreign king is reminiscent of the stories of Joseph in Genesis. The placement of the book of Daniel in the Christian canon, however, leads most people to associate it with the prophetic literature. That it is a relatively short book with a male name makes it easy to associate it with the individual books that make up the Book of the Twelve.

The most famous parts of Daniel, of course, are the story of Daniel in the lions' den and the story of the three young men who are cast into the furnace for refusing to obey an official decree to worship a Babylonian god. These two stories sit within a series of fascinating tales about faithful young Jews living in Babylon during the period of the exile. Like the stories of Joseph in Genesis 37–50 and Esther in the book that carries her name, these stories are likely intended to encourage other young Jews dispersed around the world to live faithfully in the context of a foreign empire. Daniel and his three friends, who are given the Babylonian names Shadrach, Meshach, and Abednego, are successful servants of the king and are appointed to high positions in the Babylonian government. Their success brings a high degree of visibility and the jealousy of competitors. In two similar stories, the three young men and then Daniel come into conflict with the Babylonian authorities because of the faithful practice of their religion. First, Shadrach, Meshach, and Abednego are thrown into a furnace because they refuse to worship a golden statue made by Nebuchadnezzar. When they are miraculously preserved from the flames, the king promotes them again and places a curse upon anyone who would utter blasphemy against the God of Israel.

Daniel continues to gain fame and power, and his story approaches a climax when King Belshazzar of Babylon hosts a massive feast that is interrupted when a mysterious hand appears and begins writing a message on the wall. Daniel is able to interpret the message as an announcement of the destruction of Belshazzar's kingdom. Belshazzar is overthrown and killed almost immediately, but Daniel survives and quickly moves to a high position in the Persian Empire that follows. Like the three young men, Daniel gets into trouble for his piety when he is observed praying to his God in violation of a royal decree. He is thrown into a den of lions, but escapes unharmed and is rewarded. Daniel's reputation as an interpreter of visions and dreams leads into the long sequence of visions that fills the remainder of the book.

Songs of a Prophetic Voice

It is fitting that Bob Dylan, the prophetic voice of his generation, would write and sing songs connected to the prophetic literature of the Old Testament. One of his best-known songs, "All Along the Watchtower," was made more famous by the great Jimi Hendrix recording and a more recent adaptation by U2. Dylan wrote this song in 1967, in the midst of the social upheaval of the civil rights movement and the anti-Vietnam War movement.[7] The song has numerous verbal connections to the poem found in Isaiah 21:1-10 in the midst of the section commonly called the "Oracles against the Nations." Among the words and phrases of the King James translation of Isaiah 21 that are directly reflected in the song are the wind, the watchtower, the princes, drinking, "a couple of horsemen," and a lion. The words, phrases, and ideas reflected in more subtle fashion are "whole nights," watching, pain, "bowed down," and dismayed. Both the song and the text convey the sense of something frightening approaching in the distance. It is frightening because it is a force that will bring social upheaval. In the Isaiah text, Babylon is being warned about its impending destruction, an act of vengeance for Babylon's treatment of Israel. In Dylan's context, the powerful establishment that supported racial segregation and the war in Vietnam is being threatened. In both cases, the growling of a large cat in the distance, the howling of the wind, and the approach of riders on horseback are signals of the approaching destruction. Dylan's audience is warned against false speech and self-deception. They are to get ready for the coming changes and, perhaps, even help usher them in. The audience in Isaiah 21 is a "threshed and winnowed one" for whom the destruction of Babylon, the great force of oppression in the world, is good news.

The song "Humble Mumble," popularized by the hip-hop duo known as OutKast, makes a specific reference to Isaiah 54:17 in its lyrics. Coming near the end of what is commonly called "Second Isaiah," this text speaks to Israel within the experience of the exile and its immediate aftermath. The first line of this verse in Isaiah encourages its Israelite audience with the promise "All weapons formed against you shall not prosper." The violent and obscene surface of "Humble Mumble" may at first obscure its thoughtful contemplation of the difficulties of life. The singer claims life is a "roller coaster" that requires determination in response. The notion in the song that one must respond violently to violent threats in order to survive is not foreign to the book of Isaiah. The question in both cases is whether this violence that includes ravaging and destruction (Isa 54:16) or "pistol whooping and choking" ("Humble Mumble") is always to be taken on a purely literal level. Alternation between destruction and redemption often characterizes the book of Isaiah. "Humble Mumble" is also characterized by multiple voices speaking to the audience and in conversation with one another. The multiple voices in both song and biblical text emphasize the contrasting images presented by their words. "Humble Mumble" itself acknowledges the apparent mixed messages for which hip-hop music is often criticized. The singer in the third verse responds to the criticism that hip-hop is "only guns and alcohol" with "Oh hell no, but yet it's that too." One wonders how the writer of Isaiah would respond to the criticism that prophetic literature is all about judgment, vengeance, and violent destruction.

Sting's "Jeremiah Blues" makes no direct reference to the book of Jeremiah other than the title. The tone of the entire song has much in common with the lament poems found in the book of Jeremiah. The first and second halves of the song both end with the singer's realization that a person accused of being a thief and tied to a tree is him. The lead into this chorus is Shakespeare's line from Macbeth, "Something wicked this way comes." The singer accuses society of wanting to "look the other way" when this happens. The song also pulls in the first half of the first sentence of Charles Dickens's novel *A Tale of Two Cities*: "It was the best of times." If the second half of the sentence, "it was the worst of times," is also implied, a sense of denial of evil is implied. The first of Jeremiah's laments, in Jeremiah 11:18–12:6, expresses many themes in common with the song. The speaker, Jeremiah, complains of being attacked and that wicked people are prospering. In both the song and the text, what is happening on the surface of society does not match what lies beneath that surface. Jeremiah specifically asks God to correct this situation, to punish the wicked and to vindicate him. In "Jeremiah Blues," it is not clear whether the "something wicked" brings deliverance to the singer while bringing destruction to his society.

Bruce Springsteen's "Black Cowboys" makes specific reference to Ezekiel's vision of the valley of bones in Ezekiel 37. The song tells the story of a boy growing up in a dangerous urban environment. His mother is protective and insists that he play inside their home, so he starts watching Western movies in the afternoons and becomes fascinated with the heroic "black cowboys" in the movies. As the boy grows into a young man, his mother's life is overtaken by economic disaster, a bad marriage, substance abuse, and despair. In the second half of the song, the young man runs away and gets on a train traveling west into the places he had seen in the movies as a child. The reference to Ezekiel 37 comes in the middle of the song at its turning point. The flood that destroys the home of the boy and his mother is likened to Ezekiel's valley of dry bones. As an image of defeat and disaster, this vision of Ezekiel has few equals. The skeletons represent the defeated army of the Israelites, which was destroyed by the Babylonian invasion of the sixth century. The response of the Israelite people to this situation appears in 37:11b when they say, "Our bones are dried up, our hope has perished, and we are cut off." The young man's escape to the west may be understood as a parallel to the reanimation of the bones in Ezekiel's vision. He imagines a new way of life arising out of the old. This new life is connected to his past and the dreams inspired by the movies he watched as a child. The song ends with a sense of ambiguity that matches the ambiguity of Ezekiel 37. At the end of the vision Ezekiel's reanimated army stands, but it never does anything. The vision simply ends at that point. In the song, the young man arrives in Oklahoma on the train, but the final line, "The moon rose and stripped the earth to its bone," tells nothing of how his new life develops there. The reference to bone in the final line clearly reminds the listener of the valley of dry bones again, but whether this is a sign of hope or a return to the despair that characterized the middle of the song is uncertain.

The band Third Day produced a song called "Gomer's Theme," which refers to the relationship between the biblical prophet Hosea and his wife Gomer. Gomer is a relatively minor narrative character in the book of Hosea, with no voice of her own. The reader sees her only through male eyes as a prostitute. The title of this song might offer hope that it provides something different, but those hopes are quickly dashed. The words of the song are presented first from the perspective of Hosea and then from God. The focus is on Gomer's unfaithfulness. Therefore, the song seems to assume that Gomer and the unnamed, unfaithful woman in Hosea 3 are the same person. While the song shifts from Hosea as betrayed husband to God as betrayed husband, in a way that matches the use of the marriage metaphor in the book of Hosea, there is no mention of Israel. In the final verse, it is still just an unnamed "her" that is the recipient of God's undeserved love. The song, like the book of Hosea, uses the threat of abandonment to force compliance with the desires of the husband. Likewise, it fails to raise issues about the problematic nature of this portrayal of God or the problematic nature of faith motivated by threat.

The Violent Femmes, a popular punk rock band in the 1980s, performed a song called "Hallowed Ground," which begins with a quotation of Hosea 9:7b: "The prophet is a fool, the spiritual man is mad, for the multitude of thine iniquity, and thy great hatred." Outside of its context in Hosea, it is not clear that this is being reported as a common saying in Israel, an attitude for which the Israelites are to be punished. The purpose of this quotation in the song is difficult to determine. The song is relatively brief and seems to refer to a time of violence and destruction. The voice or voices in the song look for a "place to hide" from the falling bombs, but find none.

Even the "hallowed ground" is destroyed. The singer claims, "My hope is in one they can't bring down," but it is not clear who this "one" is and whether the hope is legitimate. The final verse speaks of burying a treasure "in hallowed ground" as a response to fear of destruction, but again it is not clear whether such a plan is effective. The divine ambivalence that characterizes much of the book of Hosea might form a helpful context for this song. God wavers in the plan to destroy Israel in the book of Hosea. The fate of the one who speaks in this song may hang in that same balance.

Don Henley's thoughtful song "End of the Innocence," co-written by Bruce Hornsby, is largely a response to the last years of the Ronald Reagan presidency and the Iran-contra scandal. The first verse is about the disruption of an innocent childhood by the breakup of a family. The second verse addresses a government scandal in parallel fashion. Both events cause the destruction of childlike innocence. The scandal involves the buying and selling of weapons, so Henley pulls the quotation from Joel 3:10, "beating plowshares into swords," to talk about the promotion of war. As discussed above, the saying in Joel 3:10 is a reversal of the saying in Isaiah 2:4 and Micah 4:3, which expresses hope for peace. The song indicates a desire to escape from the disappointment of brokenness in both family and nation. The escape appears to be a romance, but the singer recognizes, or admits, that this romance will lead to a loss of innocence as well. The final verse raises questions about how innocence might be remembered and the role it might continue to play in our lives even after it has been lost. The prophetic literature of the Old Testament, because it is crisis literature, confronts a loss of innocence, but it also promotes a desire to regain innocence. The hope for a peaceful future expressed in the Isaiah and Micah form of the "swords and plowshares" saying contains at least the seeds for what later becomes an apocalyptic vision of a world where evil has been defeated and expelled. Don Henley's song is nostalgic, still looking back toward an innocence of the past, without turning to gaze forward at what might lie in the future.

Paul Simon's "Jonah" approaches the popular tale of the prophet swallowed by a fish with an appropriate playfulness. The singer of this song is a musician preparing to perform in a bar. He represents countless musicians playing in small places trying to make it big. The chorus of the song compares the life of a traveling musician to Jonah. Having heard that Jonah was "swallowed by a whale," the singer responds that there is "no truth to that tale." Instead he contends that Jonah was "swallowed by a song." In the second verse a little bit of desperation sets in as the singer chases elusive dreams. He vows to give it "one more year." The desperation of this verse may correspond to the desperation of Jonah as he says his prayer from the belly of the fish in Jonah 2. The lonely performer is captive to his music, hoping to escape to the world of fame and riches. In the third verse the voice shifts toward that of an observer who speaks of "all the boys who came along carrying soft guitars," and the song ends with a question, "Do you wonder where those boys have gone?" It is likely accidental, but intriguing nonetheless, that the book of Jonah also ends with a question when God asks Jonah, "Should I not have compassion on Nineveh, the great city, in which there are 120,000 people who do not know their right hand from their left, and many cattle?" Both questions resonate with a sense of identity. What is the role of a prophet? What is the role of an artist? Is this identity tied up in results?

A different reference to Jonah appears in Patti Smith's "Up There Down There," a mysterious song filled with religious imagery. The opening verse draws a contrast between the fiery sky, filled by the sun, and the depths of the ocean "where Jonah wails." This is a specific reference to Jonah's prayer in the belly of the fish in Jonah 2. Like the prophetic books, this song seems to contain multiple voices. Many of the images play with the distinction between heaven above and earth below, questioning the extent to which the two might be joined together. The portrait of Jonah in the depths is filled with conflict. Though the song refers to the reeds that wrap around and threaten to drown him, it also says he is "in the healing water." The song moves toward the final verses where boundaries and distinctions between heaven and earth are abolished. The image of "communion" enters the song and "up there, down there" becomes "everywhere." The prayer of Jonah in chapter 2 of the book does not fully resolve the divide between God's graceful purpose and Jonah's vengeful wishes, but helps begin to overcome it. Jonah's wailing in the first verse of "Up There Down There" may also serve as an initial connection between the desires of heaven and the struggles of humanity on earth.

The Beastie Boys' "Shadrach" possesses the tantalizing lack of coherence that characterizes much hip-hop music. There are a lot of religious images sprinkled throughout the song, but it is hard to tell whether there is an intended religious message. As each verse ends with the shouting of the names of the three young men from the book of Daniel—"Shadrach, Meshach, Abednego"—these three are being compared in some way to the members of this rapping trio. Like the biblical trio, they resist expectations. They express a hope for God's approval and acceptance in the line "And the man upstairs, I hope he cares." They refuse to be coerced into conventional behavior; however, the morality of the lifestyle expressed in parts of the song can be troubling. The honest attempt to hang on to their own identity resonates with the biblical story of the three friends in Daniel. Whether their behavior is constructive or destructive in relation to others is an issue that does not seem to be considered. This sort of self-centered, individualistic faith is common in the modern world. It is also an issue raised by the book of Daniel as it ponders the meaning of being a faithful Jew in the Diaspora.

"The handwriting was on the wall" is one of those common English expressions whose users are often unaware of its origins in the Bible. It has come to mean that something is a foregone conclusion.[8] This meaning is not inconsistent with the story in Daniel 5, in which the mysterious hand produces a message on the wall that announces the downfall of King Belshazzar and the Babylonian Empire. An adaptation of this saying appears in John Fogerty's "*Déja Vu* All Over Again." Given the publication date of 2004, the "war that has no end" is undoubtedly the Iraq war. The singer despairs, "Day by day we count the dead and dying . . . ," and "Day after day another Momma's crying." This is a story he has heard before. The "writing on the wall" in Daniel is a message with a foregone conclusion of defeat and destruction. Unfortunately, too many failed to see the writing. Therefore, the same thing is happening "all over again." This sounds like a recollection of past wars like Vietnam that received initial support from the public but turned into situations that could have no good end. Fogerty plays with the redundant phrase made famous by Yogi Berra to express the frustration of watching bad history repeat itself.

Summary and Questions for Reflection

The prophetic literature of the Old Testament confronts a vast range of theological, social, and political issues. Isaiah struggles with Israel's treatment of the weakest members of its society, Jeremiah rails against idolatry, and Amos cries out for a greater sense of economic justice. While much popular music is related to issues such as romance and personal struggles, it has also been a vehicle for artists to express their views and concerns about larger issues. Therefore, it is not surprising that there are significant points of intersection between the prophetic literature and modern popular music. Here are some questions to help you explore that intersection further.

(1) One of the primary themes of Bob Dylan's "All Along the Watchtower" is this sense of something frightening in the distance that is coming and cannot be stopped. This "something" or movement will bring incredible changes in the lives of people, and Dylan even encourages us to help usher in those changes. Can you think of a "revolution" that is coming in your context socially over the next couple of decades? Changes in economic systems, job security, educational opportunities, things that will level the playing field for some while tilting in new ways for others? Does that scare you? Does it excite you? Talk about some of the changes you think are coming—for example, changes in genetics and medicine. Are they good or bad? Is there something coming in your personal life that you feel you can't stop? Is there a way to help make the change positive for you and those you love over time? What part does God play in this inevitability of change?

(2) The issue of the use of violence to overcome violence has been raised in both the songs we mentioned here and the texts to which they refer. How do you feel about violence for violence on its surface? Doesn't at least some of history and perhaps even your own personal experience support this statement? When you consider a conflict such as World War II, do you agree with the argument that taking up arms was the only way to save the world? How do we bring the Jesus story to that dialogue? To you, was Jesus a pacifist? If not, was he at least a preacher of nonviolent responses to violent oppression? If so, how do we know when violence is appropriate as a means of bringing about social equality and justice for all?

(3) "Gomer's Theme," Third Day's treatment of the story of Hosea and his wife Gomer, brings to mind the complex issues surrounding faithfulness and commitment both metaphorically to God and to each other in life. Read the story out loud to a group of friends and then listen to the song together. Did they capture the essence of the conflict in the story? There have been some critiques put forth in this chapter about what the song does and does not do. Do you agree with them? Is there an alternative hearing of the song that you could offer? What does the story say about the nature of God? What does the story say about the nature of humanity? Does God bear any responsibility for the nature of humanity as presented in the Hosea story and the song "Gomer's Theme"?

(4) Consider the song "End of the Innocence." What do you make of the loss of innocence in your own life? When did it happen? Is it still happening? How much of it centers on intimate relationships and how much of it centers on larger community and contextual factors that force us to become people we might not choose to be or to do things we might not choose to do? Much is made of regaining one's innocence and taking care of the "inner child" in all of us. Is that truly possible? If so, how do you do that? How does one live in a healthy balance between mature acceptance of the way the world is and hopeful innocence about how the world should be?

(5) This chapter has been rich with examples of artists and prophets crying out about the problems they see in the world and how to make things better. Songs and texts are both rich with metaphor and pleading, challenging us to discover what part we can play in leaving the world better than we found it. Do any of the songs resonate with you more than others? Do you listen to any of them and feel moved to be a catalyst of change? Do they express your feelings about social and cultural issues that also connect deeply to your private and personal needs and longings? Would you be willing to create something that describes the way you see the world, perhaps a poem or a song or a work of art or even a social statement of protest? How can your needs and thoughts be expressed to others through something artistic and challenging?

(6) What other songs can you think of that have references to these biblical stories? What other questions came to mind as you were reading and discussing this section? If there were one concept or thought encountered in this part of the Bible that would cause you to live and be differently than you are now, what would it be and what will you do about it?

Notes

[1] The story of the restoration is told in the book of Ezra-Nehemiah. This account, however, does not provide a full chronology that is easy to follow, and there are no other extensive sources of information about the period. For a fuller discussion of the book of Ezra-Nehemiah, its literary development, and its difficulties, see Mark McEntire, *Dangerous Worlds: Living and Dying in Biblical Texts* (Macon GA: Smyth & Helwys, 2004), 91-108.

[2] The stark nature of this shift causes many interpreters to label Isaiah 40–55 as "Second Isaiah." Another shift that is not quite so striking has resulted in a common designation of Isaiah 56–66 as "Third Isaiah."

[3] See the discussion of the literary patterns present in the Book of the Twelve in John H. Tullock and Mark McEntire, *The Old Testament Story*, 7th ed. (Upper Saddle River NJ: Prentice Hall, 2004), 190-92.

[4] In this way, the Book of the Twelve matches the book of Isaiah, in which the prophet appears only occasionally as a narrative character. There are a number of similarities between the book of Hosea and the beginning of the book of Isaiah, including these prophetic narratives, which may explain why the book of Hosea is placed first in the Book of the Twelve.

[5] For a rigorous and thorough discussion of the issues related to the use in the prophetic literature of marriage as a metaphor for God's relationship to Israel, see Gerlinde Baumann, *Love and Violence: Marriage as Metaphor for the Relationship between YHWH and Israel in the Prophetic Books* (Collegeville MN: Liturgical Press, 2003).

[6] Most of the first half of the book of Daniel is actually written in Aramaic rather than Hebrew. Aramaic is a language closely related to Hebrew which was the official language of the Babylonian Empire. Among other things, the change in language serves as a literary device to emphasize the foreign setting of the stories in the first half of Daniel.

[7] See the discussion of this song and an accompanying pedagogical model in Mark McEntire, "Isaiah and Bob Dylan on the Watchtower," in *Teaching the Bible: Practical Strategies for Classroom Discussion*, ed. Mark Roncace and Patrick Gray (Atlanta: Society of Biblical Literature, 2005), 173-74.

[8] See the discussion of this saying and its popular usage in Michael J. Gilmour, *Tangled Up in the Bible: Bob Dylan and Scripture* (New York: Continuum, 2004), 20.

Conclusion

A Personal Retrospective

I began working with popular music in my biblical studies classes about six years ago. Once I accumulated a significant collection of songs, I entertained the idea of writing a book on the subject. For a couple of years, the shape of such a book would not emerge clearly in my mind. I began to notice the way in which the interests of songwriters clustered around certain figures, stories, and images in the Old Testament, such as Eden, the promised land, Moses, Samson and Delilah, and Jezebel. Thus, I began working with the idea of forming the book around those clusters.

At the same time, my interest in understanding the Old Testament in terms of whole books as literary works of art was coming into clearer focus. I was concerned that shaping the book around clusters of songs would fragment the Old Testament, giving attention to isolated texts at the expense of the larger contours of the whole Old Testament and the books of which it is composed. This is a force I had been struggling against in my other work with the Old Testament text. Finally, I decided to begin each chapter with a discussion of the related biblical texts, beginning with their broader shapes— the whole books in which they present themselves. I then attempted to move toward a presentation of the localized texts involved in the songs discussed in each chapter.

As the various chapters began to come together and more songs were added here and there, the book seemed to be becoming something closer to a musical tour through the Old Testament. While the clusters mentioned above were still present and visible, they had become fairly well connected by the sprinkling of songs that lay between each of them. This was a happy realization, as I became aware that I was working with the Bible in the way in which I had become accustomed in recent years. In the finished product, the natural shape of the biblical text seems to have asserted itself and found its rightful place as the force that undergirds and surrounds the discussion.

Popular music continues to play a decisive role in modern American culture. It both reflects and forms the movement of our collective life as a society. There has been a tendency, of course, for each established generation to bewail the music of the next generation as it grows up. Popular music seems to be the driving force that persistently pushes on the boundaries of established societal identities and cultural norms. At the same time, each new generation for the last half century has expressed a desire to retain the music of a past generation. When I was in high school, we had '50s parties where we dressed up like the characters on the television show *Happy Days* and listened and danced to Elvis Presley, Buddy Holly, Chuck Berry, and Chubby Checker. My own teenage children recently went to an '80s party, which made me feel terribly old, but it is a surpassing pleasure when a song that was popular when I was in high school comes on the car radio and they know the words. Thus, popular music moves not only relentlessly forward, but backward as well.

The ultimate movement against the forward march of time comes when our music reaches far back into the depths of our remembered experience to our earliest cultural repositories, like the Bible. A vast gulf of time, geographical distance, and cultural difference lies between us and the groups of people that produced the literature we find in the Old Testament. How is that gulf spanned in the modern act of reading an ancient text? How does a creation story that assumes a flat earth and a map limited to the land between Ethiopia and Mesopotamia continue to communicate to those of us who have traveled around the globe and seen close-up photographs of Mars?

Perhaps more than many others, the songwriters and singers who have made an appearance in the preceding pages are aware, on some level, of the Bible's creative capacity to pose questions. The Bible is at its best when we allow it to perform this great task. When we force the Bible to yield answers to these questions, the answers often feel quaint, stilted, distant, and even inappropriate. The strange story of Noah and his sons in Genesis 9:18-29 offers us no useful information about the modern world. What is to be gained from understanding that the descendants of one son are cursed to be slaves of another because of some poorly defined, barely remembered offense of the distant past? But when we let this story ask, "How should you think about and act toward people who are different from you?" we approach the urgency intended by its original author.

The first half of the new documentary film about Bob Dylan, *No Direction Home*, by Martin Scorsese aired last night on public television. I expected something from the film might end up in this closing reflection, but I was taken by surprise. Despite my fascination with Dylan, the most powerful moment in the first half of the film was the mesmerizing clip of Billie Holiday singing "Strange Fruit." The song was written in the 1930s by "Lewis Allen," the pseudonym used by a New York school teacher named Abel Meeropol. "Strange Fruit" may not fulfill the criteria I established for inclusion in this book, but the subtle resonances between its lyrics and the complex of stories in Genesis 2–4, along with the striking discovery of its writer's first name, give it an irresistible pull.[1] Is the eating of the fruit from the forbidden tree at the center of the garden the beginning of our end or the end of our beginning? It is followed almost immediately by the first story of murder. While fruit sends us out into the world east of Eden, will the "strange fruit" of lynched bodies be our end? The second verse of the song presents a stunning pair of contrasts, one visual and the other olfactory. Stories and music invade all of our senses. The power of story and the power of song to move us back and forth between pleasure and pain explodes at the creative junctures where our oldest stories and our newest artistic visions collide.

Note

[1] This song was the subject of its own documentary film. For more information about it, see http://www.pbs.org/independentlens/strangefruit/film.html.

Using the Song Charts

We have organized the songs included in the book into three indexes that we hope you will use as valuable reference tools. They all contain basically the same information, but are sorted differently, one by song title, one by artist, and one by biblical reference, each with a listing of the chapter of this book in which the song is found. We wanted the book to be used by a wide range of people with various interests and needs. As such, the biblical reference index is alphabetized by the first three letters of the book of the Bible to which the song refers. Also, any listing that does not include a chapter number is because the song refers to broader themes found in that biblical book, not necessarily one specific reference to a verse or chapter.

Finally, we have found certain websites to be invaluable in our research and hope that you might find them useful as well. First, www.allmusic.com may be the most in-depth popular song index on the Internet. Also of great help was www.rollingstone.com as well as the performance rights organizations' websites at www.bmi.com, www.ascap.com, and www.sesac.com. We also referred to official artists' websites as well. You can easily find those by searching for an artist's name on the major Internet search engines such as www.google.com or www.yahoo.com. We were unable to include lyrics due to copyright limitations, but those too can be found with simple web searches based on the song title and artist.

CHART A: Songs by Title

Song Title	Artist/Album
"Adam and Eve"	Ani Difranco/ *Dilate*
"Adam Raised a Cain"	Bruce Springsteen/ *Darkness on the Edge of Town*
"Adam's Apple"	Aerosmith/ *Toys in the Attic*
"Against the Grain"	Garth Brooks/ *Ropin' the Wind*
"All Along the Watchtower"	Bob Dylan/ *John Wesley Harding*
"Bang the Drum Slowly"	Emmylou Harris/ *Red Dirt Girl*
"Banner Year"	Five Iron Frenzy/ *Our Newest Album Ever*
"Beautiful Day"	U2/ *All That You Can't Leave Behind*
"Before the Deluge"	Jackson Browne/ *Late for the Sky*
"Black Cowboys"	Bruce Springsteen/ *Devils and Dust*
"Blowin' in the Wind"	Bob Dylan/ *Freewheelin*
"Bullet the Blue Sky"	U2/ *Joshua Tree, The*
"Coat of Many Colors"	Dolly Parton/ *Coat of Many Colors*
"Creeping Death"	Metallica/ *Ride the Lightning*
"Crossfire"	Stevie Ray Vaughn and Double Trouble/ *Instep*
"Cumbersome"	Seven Mary Three/ *American Standard*
"Deja' Vu All Over Again"	John Fogerty/ *Déjà vu All Over Again*
"Delilah"	Tom Jones/ *Green Green Grass of Home*
"Dust in the Wind"	Kansas/ *Point of No Return*
"Eden"	10,000 Maniacs/ *Our Time in Eden*
"End of the Innocence"	Don Henley/ *The End of the Innocence*
"Exodus"	Bob Marley and the Wailers/ *Exodus*
"Final Hour"	Lauryn Hill/ *The Miseducation of Lauryn Hill*
"Fire"	Bruce Springsteen and the E Street Band/ *Live 1975-85*
"Flood"	Jars of Clay/ *Jars of Clay*
"Forever Loving Jah"	Bob Marley and the Wailers/ *Uprising*
"Forty"	U2/ *War*
"Gangsta's Paradise"	Coolio/ *Gangsta's Paradise*
"Gates of Eden, The"	Bob Dylan/ *Bringing It All Back Home*
"Gomer's Theme"	Third Day/ *Conspiracy #5*
"Hallelujah"	Leonard Cohen/ *Various Positions*
"Hallowed Ground"	Violent Femmes, The/ *Hallowed Ground*
"Highway 61 Revisited"	Bob Dylan/ *Highway 61 Revisited*
"Humble Mumble"	OutKast/ *Stankonia*
"Isaac and Abraham"	Joan Baez/ *Play Me Backwards*

Composer(s)	Label/Year	Bib. Reference	Chapter
Ani DiFranco	Righteous Babe/1996	Gen 2	1
Bruce Springsteen	Columbia/1978	Gen 4	1
Steven Tyler	Sony/1975	Gen 3–4	1
Bruce Bouton, Larry Cordle, Carl Jackson	Capitol/1991	Gen 6–8	2
Bob Dylan	Columbia/1967	Isa 21	7
Guy Clark, Emmylou Harris	Elektra/2000	Gen 3	1
Scott Kerr, Reese Roper	SaraBellum/1997	Song 2	6
Bono, U2	Interscope/2000	Gen 8–9	2
Jackson Browne	Asylum/1974	Gen 5–6	1
Bruce Springsteen	Columbia/2005	Ezek 37	7
Bob Dylan	Columbia/1963	Gen 8	2
Bono, Adam Clayton, The Edge, Larry Mullen, Jr.	Island/1987	Gen 32	3
Dolly Parton	Buddha/1971	Gen 37–50	3
Cliff Burton, Kirk Hammett, James Hetfield, Lars Ulrich	Elektra/1984	Exod 12	4
B. Carter, Ruth Ellsworth, Chris Layton, Tommy Shannon, Reese Wynans	Epic-Legacy/1989	Exod 21	4
J. Pollock, J. A. Ross	Atlantic/1995	1 Sam 17	5
John Fogerty	Geffen/2004	Dan 5	7
Barry Mason, Les Reed	Polygram/1967	Judg 16	4
Kerry Livgren	Kirshner/1977	Eccl 1–12	6
Jerome Augustyniak, Robert Buck, Dennis Drew, Steve Gustafson, Natalie Merchant	Elektra/1992	Gen 2	1
Don Henley, Bruce Hornsby	Geffin/1989	Joel 3	7
Bob Marley	Tuff Gong/1977	Exod	4
Lauryn Hill	Ruffhouse/1998	Ps 73	6
Bruce Springsteen	Columbia/1986	Judg 16	5
Dan Haseltine, Charlie Lowell, Steve Mason, Matt Odmark	Essential(Jive)/1995	Gen 6–8	2
Bob Marley	Tuff Gong/1980	Ps 1	6
U2	Island/1983	Ps 40	6
Coolio (Artis Ivey)	Tommy Boy/1995	Ps 23	6
Bob Dylan	Columbia/1965	Gen 3	1
Mac Powell, Third Day	Reunion—Silvertone/1997	Hos	7
Leonard Cohen	Columbia/1985	1 Sam 16	5
Gordon Gano	Slash/Rhino/1984	Hos 9	7
Bob Dylan	Columbia/1965	Gen 22	3
Andre Benjamin, Antwan Andre Patton, David Sheats, Erica Wright	Le Face/2000	Isa 54	7
Joan Baez, Kenny Greenberg, Wally Wilson	Virgin/1992	Gen 22	3

SONG TITLE	ARTIST/ALBUM
"Jacob's Ladder"	Bruce Hornsby and the Range/ *Songs from the Southside*
"Jeremiah Blues"	Sting/ *The Soul Cages*
"Jezebel"	10,000 Maniacs/ *Our Time in Eden*
"Jezebel"	Chely Wright/ *Never Love You Enough*
"Jonah"	Paul Simon/ *In Concert* (Video)
"Joseph and the Amazing Technicolor Dreamcoat"	Toronto Musical Review (Cast Recording)
"Kenaniah"	Petra/ *This Means War*
"Man Gave Names to All the Animals"	Bob Dylan/ *Slow Train Coming*
"Man on the Moon"	REM/ *Automatic for the People*
"Meaningless"	Sixpence None the Richer/ *The Fatherless and the Widow*
"Mercy Seat, The"	Nick Cave and the Bad Seeds/ *Tender Prey*
"Moses"	Patti Griffin/ *Living with Ghosts*
"My Brother Esau"	Grateful Dead, The/ *In the Dark*
"Noah's Dove"	10,000 Maniacs/ *Our Time in Eden*
"Promised Land"	Bruce Springsteen/ *Darkness on the Edge of Town*
"Rain on the Scarecrow"	John Mellencamp/ *Scarecrow*
"Ramble on Rose"	Grateful Dead, The/ *Europe '72*
"Redemption Song"	Bob Marley and the Wailers/ *Uprising*
"River of Dreams"	Billy Joel/ *River of Dreams*
"Rock and Roll Creation"	Spinal Tap/ *This is Spinal Tap*
"Samson and Delilah"	Grateful Dead, The/ *Terrapin Station*
"Shadrach"	Beastie Boys, The/ *Paul's Boutique*
"Sin Wagon"	Dixie Chicks/ *Fly*
"Sire of Sorrows"	Joni Mitchell/ *Turbulent Indigo*
"Song of Solomon, The"	Kate Bush/ *The Red Shoes*
"Standing Still"	Jewel/ *This Way*
"Tripping Billies"	Dave Matthews Band, The/ *Remember Two Things*
"Turn Turn Turn"	Byrds, The/ *Turn, Turn, Turn*
"Two Step"	Dave Matthews Band, The/ *Crash*
"Up There Down There"	Patti Smith/ *Dream of Life*

Composer(s)	Label/Year	Bib.Reference	Chapter
Bruce Hornsby, John Hornsby	RCA/1988	Gen 28	3
Sting, Dominic Miller	A&M/1991	Jer 11	7
Natalie Merchant	Elektra/1992	1 Kgs 16	5
Jay Demarcus, Marcus Hummon	MCA/2002	1 Kgs 16	5
Paul Simon	Warner Reprise/1972	Jonah	7
Andrew Lloyd Webber, Tim Rice	Lake Shore/1996	Gen 37–50	3
Bob Hartman, Danny Kingen, John Lawry	Star Song/1987	1 Chr 15	5
Bob Dylan	Columbia/1979	Gen 2	1
Bill Berry, Peter Buck, Mike Mills, Michael Stipe	Warner Brothers/1992	Deut 32	4
Matt Slocum	Flying Tart/1994	Eccl	6
Nick Cave, Mick Harvey	Mute/1988	Exod 37	4
Patti Griffin	A&M/1996	Exod 14–15	4
John Perry Barlow, Bob Weir	Arista/1987	Gen 25	3
Natalie Merchant	Elektra/1992	Gen 6–8	2
Bruce Springsteen	Columbia/1978	Exod	4
George M. Green, John Mellencamp	Mercury/1985	Exod	4
Jerry Garcia, Robert Hunter	Warner Brothers/1972	Josh 5–6	5
Bob Marley	Tuff Gong /1980	Gen 37–Exod	3
Billy Joel	Columbia/1993	Exod	4
Christopher Guest, Michael McKean, Rob Reiner, Harry Shearer	Polydor/1984	Gen 1	1
Traditional	Arista/1977	Judg 13–16	5
Beastie Boys, Dust Brothers	Capital/1989	Dan 3	7
Natalie Maines, Emily Robison, Stephony Smith	Monument/1999	Judg 16	5
Joni Mitchell	Reprise/1994	Job 1–4	6
Kate Bush	Columbia/1993	Song 2	6
Jewel Kilcher, Rick Nowels	Atlantic/2001	Exod 3	4
Dave Matthews	RCA/1993	Eccl	6
Pete Seeger	Columbia/1965	Eccl 3	6
Dave Matthews	RCA/1996	Gen 6–8	2
Fred "Sonic" Smith, Patti Smith	Arista/1988	Jonah 2	7

CHART B: Songs by Artist

ARTIST/ALBUM	SONG TITLE
10,000 Maniacs/ *Our Time in Eden*	"Eden"
10,000 Maniacs/ *Our Time in Eden*	"Noah's Dove"
10,000 Maniacs/ *Our Time in Eden*	"Jezebel"
Aerosmith/ *Toys in the Attic*	"Adam's Apple"
Ani Difranco/ *Dilate*	"Adam and Eve"
Beastie Boys, The/ *Paul's Boutique*	"Shadrach"
Billy Joel/ *River of Dreams*	"River of Dreams"
Bob Dylan/ *Freewheelin*	"Blowin' in the Wind"
Bob Dylan/ *Bringing It All Back Home*	"Gates of Eden, The"
Bob Dylan/ *Slow Train Coming*	"Man Gave Names to All the Animals"
Bob Dylan/ *Highway 61 Revisited*	"Highway 61 Revisited"
Bob Dylan/ *John Wesley Harding*	"All Along the Watchtower"
Bob Marley and the Wailers/ *Uprising*	"Forever Loving Jah"
Bob Marley and the Wailers/ *Exodus*	"Exodus"
Bob Marley and the Wailers/ *Uprising*	"Redemption Song"
Bruce Hornsby and the Range/ *Songs from the Southside*	"Jacob's Ladder"
Bruce Springsteen/ *Darkness on the Edge of Town*	"Adam Raised a Cain"
Bruce Springsteen/ *Darkness on the Edge of Town*	"Promised Land"
Bruce Springsteen/ *Devils and Dust*	"Black Cowboys"
Bruce Springsteen and the E Street Band/ *Live 1975-85*	"Fire"
Byrds, The/ *Turn, Turn, Turn*	"Turn Turn Turn"
Chely Wright/ *Never Love You Enough*	"Jezebel"
Coolio/ *Gangsta's Paradise*	"Gangsta's Paradise"
Dave Matthews Band, The/ *Crash*	"Two Step"
Dave Matthews Band, The/ *Remember Two Things*	"Tripping Billies"
Dixie Chicks/ *Fly*	"Sin Wagon"
Dolly Parton/ *Coat of Many Colors*	"Coat of Many Colors"
Don Henley/ *The End of the Innocence*	"End of the Innocence"
Emmylou Harris/ *Red Dirt Girl*	"Bang the Drum Slowly"
Five Iron Frenzy/ *Our Newest Album Ever*	"Banner Year"
Garth Brooks/ *Ropin' the Wind*	"Against the Grain"
Grateful Dead, The/ *Europe '72*	"Ramble on Rose"
Grateful Dead, The/ *Terrapin Station*	"Samson and Delilah"
Grateful Dead, The/ *In the Dark*	"My Brother Esau"
Jackson Browne/ *Late for the Sky*	"Before the Deluge"
Jars of Clay/ *Jars of Clay*	"Flood"
Jewel/ *This Way*	"Standing Still"
Joan Baez/ *Play Me Backwards*	"Isaac and Abraham"
John Fogerty/ *Déjà vu All Over Again*	"Déja' Vu All Over Again"

Composer(s)	Label/Year	Bib.Reference	Chapter
Jerome Augustyniak, Robert Buck, Dennis Drew, Steve Gustafson, Natalie Merchant	Elektra/1992	Gen 2	1
Natalie Merchant	Elektra/1992	Gen 6–8	2
Natalie Merchant	Elektra/1992	1 Kgs 16	5
Steven Tyler	Sony/1975	Gen 3–4	1
Ani DiFranco	Righteous Babe/ 1996	Gen 2	1
Beastie Boys, Dust Brothers	Capital/1989	Dan 3	7
Billy Joel	Columbia/1993	Exod	4
Bob Dylan	Columbia/1963	Gen 8	2
Bob Dylan	Columbia/1965	Gen 3	1
Bob Dylan	Columbia/1979	Gen 2	1
Bob Dylan	Columbia/1965	Gen 22	3
Bob Dylan	Columbia/1967	Isa 21	7
Bob Marley	Tuff Gong/1980	Ps 1	6
Bob Marley	Tuff Gong/1977	Exod	4
Bob Marley	Tuff Gong /1980	Gen 37–Exod	3
Bruce Hornsby, John Hornsby	RCA/1988	Gen 28	3
Bruce Springsteen	Columbia 1978	Gen 4	2
Bruce Springsteen	Columbia/1978	Exod	4
Bruce Springsteen	Columbia/2005	Ezek 37	7
Bruce Springsteen	Columbia/1986	Judg 16	5
Pete Seeger	Columbia/1965	Eccl 3	6
Jay Demarcus, Marcus Hummon	MCA/2002	1 Kgs 16	5
Coolio (Artis Ivey)	Tommy Boy/1995	Ps 23	6
Dave Matthews	RCA/1996	Gen 6–8	2
Dave Matthews	RCA/1993	Eccl	6
Natalie Maines, Emily Robison, Stephony Smith	Monument/1999	Judg 16	5
Dolly Parton	Buddha/1971	Gen 37–50	3
Don Henley, Bruce Hornsby	Geffin/1989	Joel 3	7
Guy Clark, Emmylou Harris	Elektra/2000	Gen 3	1
Scott Kerr, Reese Roper	SaraBellum/1997	Song 2	6
Bruce Bouton, Larry Cordle, Carl Jackson	Capitol/1991	Gen 6–8	2
Jerry Garcia, Robert Hunter	Warner Brothers/1972	Josh 5–6	5
Traditional	Arista/1977	Judg 13–16	5
John Perry Barlow, Bob Weir	Arista/1987	Gen 25	3
Jackson Browne	Asylum/1974	Gen 5–6	1
Dan Haseltine, Charlie Lowell, Steve Mason, Matt Odmark	Essential(Jive)/1995	Gen 6–8	2
Jewel Kilcher, Rick Nowels	Atlantic/2001	Exod 3	4
Joan Baez, Kenny Greenberg, Wally Wilson	Virgin/1992	Gen 22	3
John Fogerty	Geffen/2004	Dan 5	7

ARTIST/ALBUM	SONG TITLE
John Mellencamp/ *Scarecrow*	"Rain on the Scarecrow"
Joni Mitchell/ *Turbulent Indigo*	"Sire of Sorrows"
Kansas/ *Point of No Return*	"Dust in the Wind"
Kate Bush/ *The Red Shoes*	"Song of Solomon, The"
Lauryn Hill/ *The Miseducation of Lauryn Hill*	"Final Hour"
Leonard Cohen/ *Various Positions*	"Hallelujah"
Metallica/ *Ride the Lightning*	"Creeping Death"
Nick Cave and the Bad Seeds/ *Tender Prey*	"Mercy Seat, The"
OutKast/ *Stankonia*	"Humble Mumble"
Patti Griffin/ *Living with Ghosts*	"Moses"
Patti Smith/ *Dream of Life*	"Up There Down There"
Paul Simon/ *In Concert* (Video)	"Jonah"
Petra/ *This Means War*	"Kenaniah"
REM/ *Automatic for the People*	"Man on the Moon"
Seven Mary Three/ *American Standard*	"Cumbersome"
Sixpence None the Richer/ *The Fatherless and the Widow*	"Meaningless"
Spinal Tap/ *This Is Spinal Tap*	"Rock and Roll Creation"
Stevie Ray Vaughn and Double Trouble/ *Instep*	"Crossfire"
Sting/ *The Soul Cages*	"Jeremiah Blues"
Third Day/ *Conspiracy #5*	"Gomer's Theme"
Tom Jones/ *Green Green Grass of Home*	"Delilah"
Toronto Musical Review (Cast Recording)	"Joseph and the Amazing Technicolor Dreamcoat"
U2/ *All That You Can't Leave Behind*	"Beautiful Day"
U2/ *Joshua Tree, The*	"Bullet the Blue Sky"
U2/ *War*	"Forty"
Violent Femmes, The/ *Hallowed Ground*	"Hallowed Ground"

COMPOSER(S)	LABEL/YEAR	BIB.REFERENCE	CHAPTER
George M. Green, John Mellencamp	Mercury/1985	Exod	4
Joni Mitchell	Reprise/1994	Job 1–4	6
Kerry Livgren	Kirshner/1977	Eccl 1–12	6
Kate Bush	Columbia/1993	Song 2	6
Lauryn Hill	Ruffhouse/1998	Ps 73	6
Leonard Cohen	Columbia/1985	1 Sam 16	5
Cliff Burton, Kirk Hammett, James Hetfield, Lars Ulrich	Elektra/1984	Exod 12	4
Nick Cave, Mick Harvey	Mute/1988	Exod 37	4
Andre Benjamin, Antwan Andre Patton, David Sheats, Erica Wright	Le Face/2000	Isa 54	7
Patti Griffin	A&M/1996	Exod 14–15	4
Fred "Sonic" Smith, Patti Smith	Arista/1988	Jonah 2	7
Paul Simon	Warner Reprise/1972	Jonah	7
Bob Hartman, Danny Kingen, John Lawry	Star Song/1987	1 Chr 15	5
Bill Berry, Peter Buck, Mike Mills, Michael Stipe	Warner Brothers/1992	Deut 32	4
J. Pollock, J. A. Ross	Atlantic/1995	1 Sam 17	5
Matt Slocum	Flying Tart/1994	Eccl	6
Christopher Guest, Michael McKean, Rob Reiner, Harry Shearer	Polydor/1984	Gen 1	1
B. Carter, Ruth Ellsworth, Chris Layton, Tommy Shannon, Reese Wynans	Epic-Legacy/1989	Exod 21	4
Sting, Dominic Miller	A&M/1991	Jer 11	7
Mac Powell, Third Day	Reunion-Silvertone/1997	Hos	7
Barry Mason, Les Reed	Polygram/1967	Judg 16	5
Andrew Lloyd Webber, Tim Rice	Lake Shore/1996	Gen 37–50	3
Bono, U2	Interscope/2000	Gen 8–9	2
Bono, Adam Clayton, The Edge, Larry Mullen, Jr.	Island/1987	Gen 32	3
U2	Island/1983	Ps 40	6
Gordon Gano	Slash/Rhino/1984	Hos 9	7

CHART C: Songs by Biblical Reference

BIB. REFERENCE	CHAPTER	SONG TITLE	COMPOSER(S)
1 Chr 15	5	"Kenaniah"	Bob Hartman, Danny Kingen, John Lawry
1 Kgs 16	5	"Jezebel"	Natalie Merchant
1 Kgs 16	5	"Jezebel"	Jay Demarcus, Marcus Hummon
1 Sam 16	5	"Hallelujah"	Leonard Cohen
1 Sam 17	5	"Cumbersome"	J. Pollock, J. A. Ross
Dan 3	7	"Shadrach"	Beastie Boys, The; Dust Brothers, The
Dan 5	7	"Deja' Vu All Over Again"	John Fogerty
Deut 32	4	"Man on the Moon"	Bill Berry, Peter Buck, Mike Mills, Michael Stipe
Eccl	6	"Meaningless"	Matt Slocum
Eccl	6	"Tripping Billies"	Dave Matthews
Eccl 1–12	6	"Dust in the Wind"	Kerry Livgren
Eccl 3	6	"Turn Turn Turn"	Pete Seeger
Exod	4	"Exodus"	Bob Marley
Exod	4	"Promised Land"	Bruce Springsteen
Exod	4	"Rain on the Scarecrow"	George M. Green, John Mellencamp
Exod	4	"River of Dreams"	Billy Joel
Exod 12	4	"Creeping Death"	Cliff Burton, Kirk Hammett, James Hetfield, Lars Ulrich
Exod 14–15	4	"Moses"	Patti Griffin
Exod 21	4	"Crossfire"	B. Carter, Ruth Ellsworth, Chris Layton, Tommy Shannon, Reese Wynans
Exod 3	4	"Standing Still"	Jewel Kilcher, Rick Nowels
Exod 37	4	"Mercy Seat, The"	Nick Cave, Mick Harvey
Ezek 37	7	"Black Cowboys"	Bruce Springsteen
Gen 1	1	"Rock and Roll Creation"	Christopher Guest, Michael McKean, Rob Reiner, Harry Shearer
Gen 2	1	"Adam and Eve"	Ani DiFranco
Gen 2	1	"Eden"	Jerome Augustyniak, Robert Buck, Dennis Drew, Steve Gustafson, Natalie Merchant
Gen 2	1	"Man Gave Names to All the Animals"	Bob Dylan
Gen 3	1	"Bang the Drum Slowly"	Guy Clark, Emmylou Harris
Gen 3	1	"Gates of Eden, The"	Bob Dylan
Gen 3–4	1	"Adam's Apple"	Steven Tyler
Gen 4	1	"Adam Raised a Cain"	Bruce Springsteen
Gen 5–6	1	"Before the Deluge "	Jackson Browne
Gen 6–8	2	"Against the Grain"	Bruce Bouton, Larry Cordle, Carl Jackson

CHART C

Artist/Album	Label/Year
Petra/ *This Means War*	Star Song/1987
10,000 Maniacs/ *Our Time in Eden*	Elektra/1992
Chely Wright/ *Never Love You Enough*	MCA/2002
Leonard Cohen/ *Various Positions*	Columbia/1985
Seven Mary Three/ *American Standard*	Atlantic/1995
Beastie Boys, The/ *Paul's Boutique*	Capital/1989
John Fogerty/ *Déjà vu All Over Again*	Geffen/2004
REM/ *Automatic for the People*	Warner Brothers/1992
Sixpence None the Richer/ *The Fatherless and the Widow*	Flying Tart/1994
Dave Matthews Band, The/ *Remember Two Things*	RCA/1993
Kansas/ *Point of No Return*	Kirshner/1977
Byrds, The/ *Turn, Turn, Turn*	Columbia/1965
Bob Marley and the Wailers/ *Exodus*	Tuff Gong/1977
Bruce Springsteen/ *Darkness on the Edge of Town*	Columbia/1978
John Mellencamp/ *Scarecrow*	Mercury/1985
Billy Joel/ *River of Dreams*	Columbia/1993
Metallica/ *Ride the Lightning*	Elektra/1984
Patti Griffin/ *Living with Ghosts*	A&M/1996
Stevie Ray Vaughn and Double Trouble/ *Instep*	Epic-Legacy/1989
Jewel/ *This Way*	Atlantic/2001
Nick Cave and the Bad Seeds/ *Tender Prey*	Mute/1988
Bruce Springsteen/ *Devils and Dust*	Columbia/2005
Spinal Tap/ *This is Spinal Tap*	Polydor/1984
Ani Difranco/ *Dilate*	Righteous Babe/ 1996
10,000 Maniacs/ *Our Time in Eden*	Elektra/1992
Bob Dylan/ *Slow Train Coming*	Columbia/1979
Emmylou Harris/ *Red Dirt Girl*	Elektra/2000
Bob Dylan/ *Bringing It All Back Home*	Columbia/1965
Aerosmith/ *Toys in the Attic*	Sony/1975
Bruce Springsteen/ *Darkness on the Edge of Town*	Columbia 1978
Jackson Browne/ *Late for the Sky*	Asylum/1974
Garth Brooks/ *Ropin' the Wind*	Capitol/1991

Bib. Reference	Chapter	Song Title	Composer(s)
Gen 6–8	2	"Flood"	Dan Haseltine, Charlie Lowell, Steve Mason, Matt Odmark
Gen 6–8	2	"Noah's Dove"	Natalie Merchant
Gen 6–8	2	"Two Step"	Dave Matthews
Gen 8	2	"Blowin' in the Wind"	Bob Dylan
Gen 8–9	2	"Beautiful Day"	Bono, U2
Gen 22	3	"Highway 61 Revisited"	Bob Dylan
Gen 22	3	"Isaac and Abraham"	Joan Baez, Kenny Greenberg, Wally Wilson
Gen 25	3	"My Brother Esau"	John Perry Barlow, Bob Weir
Gen 28	3	"Jacob's Ladder"	Bruce Hornsby, John Hornsby
Gen 32	3	"Bullet the Blue Sky"	Bono, Adam Clayton, The Edge, Larry Mullen, Jr.
Gen 37–50	3	"Coat of Many Colors"	Dolly Parton
Gen 37–50	3	"Joseph and the Amazing Technicolor Dreamcoat"	Andrew Lloyd Webber, Tim Rice
Gen 37–Exod	3	"Redemption Song"	Bob Marley
Hos	7	"Gomer's Theme"	Mac Powell, Third Day
Hos 9	7	"Hallowed Ground"	Gordon Gano
Isa 21	7	"All Along the Watchtower"	Bob Dylan
Isa 54	7	"Humble Mumble"	Andre Benjamin, Antwan Andre Patton, David Sheats, Erica Wright
Jer 11	7	"Jeremiah Blues"	Sting, Dominic Miller
Job 1–4	6	"Sire of Sorrows"	Joni Mitchell
Joel 3	7	"End of the Innocence"	Don Henley, Bruce Hornsby
Jonah	7	"Jonah"	Paul Simon
Jonah 2	7	"Up There Down There"	Fred "Sonic" Smith, Patti Smith
Josh 5–6	5	"Ramble on Rose"	Jerry Garcia, Robert Hunter
Judg 13–16	5	"Samson and Delilah"	Traditional
Judg 16	5	"Delilah"	Barry Mason, Les Reed
Judg 16	5	"Fire"	Bruce Springsteen
Judg 16	5	"Sin Wagon"	Natalie Maines, Emily Robison, Stephony Smith
Ps 1	6	"Forever Loving Jah"	Bob Marley
Ps 23	6	"Gangsta's Paradise"	Coolio (Artis Ivey)
Ps 40	6	"Forty"	U2
Ps 73	6	"Final Hour"	Lauryn Hill
Song 2	6	"Banner Year"	Scott Kerr, Reese Roper
Song 2	6	"Song of Solomon, The"	Kate Bush

CHART C

ARTIST/ALBUM	LABEL/YEAR
Jars of Clay/ *Jars of Clay*	Essential(Jive)/1995
10,000 Maniacs/ *Our Time in Eden*	Elektra/1992
Dave Matthews Band, The/ *Crash*	RCA/1996
Bob Dylan/ *Freewheelin*	Columbia/1963
U2/ *All That You Can't Leave Behind*	Interscope/2000
Bob Dylan/ *Highway 61 Revisited*	Columbia/1965
Joan Baez/ *Play Me Backwards*	Virgin/1992
Grateful Dead, The/ *In the Dark*	Arista/1987
Bruce Hornsby and the Range/ *Songs from the Southside*	RCA/1988
U2/ *Joshua Tree, The*	Island/1987
Dolly Parton/ *Coat of Many Colors*	Buddha/1971
Toronto Musical Review (Cast Recording)	Lake Shore/1996
Bob Marley and the Wailers/ *Uprising*	Tuff Gong /1980
Third Day/ *Conspiracy #5*	Reunion-Silvertone/1997
Violent Femmes, The/ *Hallowed Ground*	Slash/Rhino/1984
Bob Dylan/ *John Wesley Harding*	Columbia/1967
Outkast/ *Stankonia*	Le Face/2000
Sting/ *The Soul Cages*	A&M/1991
Joni Mitchell/ *Turbulent Indigo*	Reprise/1994
Don Henley / *The End of the Innocence*	Geffin/1989
Paul Simon/ *In Concert* (Video)	Warner Reprise/1972
Patti Smith/ *Dream of Life*	Arista/1988
Grateful Dead, The/ *Europe '72*	Warner Brothers/1972
Grateful Dead, The/ *Terrapin Station*	Arista/1977
Tom Jones/ *Green Green Grass of Home*	Polygram/1967
Bruce Springsteen and the E Street Band/ *Live 1975-85*	Columbia/1986
Dixie Chicks/ *Fly*	Monument/1999
Bob Marley and the Wailers/ *Uprising*	Tuff Gong/1980
Coolio/ *Gangsta's Paradise*	Tommy Boy/1995
U2/ *War*	Island/1983
Lauryn Hill/ *The Miseducation of Lauryn Hill*	Ruffhouse/1998
Five Iron Frenzy/ *Our Newest Album Ever*	SaraBellum/1997
Kate Bush/ *The Red Shoes*	Columbia/1993

Suggested Further Reading

This is a list of books that give excellent attention to the literary aspects of the biblical text and the ways that it has interacted with other aspects of human culture. There are also a few books addressing the intersection between the Bible and popular music and the use of this intersection in teaching.

The Old Testament and the Bible in General
Alter, Robert. *The Art of Biblical Narrative.* New York: Basic Books, 1981.
Jones, Gareth Lloyd. *The Bones of Joseph: From the Ancient Texts to the Modern Church.* Grand Rapids: William B. Eerdmans Publishing Co., 1997.
Kirsch, Jonathan. *The Harlot by the Side of the Road: Forbidden Tales of the Bible.* New York: Ballantine Books, 1997.
Levison John and Priscilla Pope-Levison, eds. *Return to Babel: Global Perspectives on the Bible.* Louisville: Westminster John Knox Press, 1999.
McEntire, Mark. *The Blood of Abel: The Violent Plot of the Hebrew Bible.* Macon GA: Mercer University Press, 1999.
———. *Dangerous Worlds: Living and Dying in Biblical Texts.* Macon GA: Smyth & Helwys Publishing, 2004.
Miles, Jack. *God: A Biography.* New York: Vintage Press, 1995.

Roncace, Mark, and Patrick Gray, eds. *Teaching the Bible: Practical Strategies for Classroom Discussion.* Atlanta: Society of Biblical Literature, 2005.

Schwartz, Regina M. *The Curse of Cain: The Violent Legacy of Monotheism.* Chicago: University of Chicago Press, 1997.

Tullock, John H., and Mark McEntire. *The Old Testament Story*, 7th ed. New York: Prentice Hall, 2005.

Genesis

Alter, Robert. *Genesis: Translation and Commentary.* New York: W. W. Norton & Co., 1996.

Brueggemann, Walter. *Genesis.* Interpretation. Atlanta: John Knox Press, 1982.

Humphreys, W. Lee. *The Character of God in the Book of Genesis: A Narrative Appraisal.* Louisville: Westminster John Knox Press, 2001.

Pagels, Elaine. *Adam, Eve, and the Serpent.* New York: Vintage Press, 1989.

Steinmetz, Devora. *From Father to Son: Kinship, Conflict and Continuity in Genesis.* Louisville: Westminster John Knox Press, 1991.

Exodus–Deuteronomy

Britt, Brian. *Rewriting Moses: The Narrative Eclipse of the Text.* London: T&T Clark, 2004.

Wright, Melanie J. *Moses in America: The Cultural Uses of Biblical Narrative.* Oxford: Oxford University Press, 2003

Joshua–Judges

Niditch, Susan. *War in the Hebrew Bible: A Study in the Ethics of Violence.* Oxford: Oxford University Press, 1993.

Schneider, Tammi J. *Judges.* Berit Olam. Collegeville MN: Liturgical Press, 2000.

Samuel–Kings–Chronicles

Alter, Robert. *The David Story: A Translation with Commentary of 1 and 2 Samuel.* New York: W. W. Norton & Co., 1999.

Gunn, David M. *The Fate of King Saul: An Interpretation of a Biblical Story.* Sheffield: Sheffield University Press, 1980.

————. *The Story of King David: Genre and Interpretation.* Sheffield: JSOT Press, 1978.

Psalms

Brown, William P. *Seeing the Psalms: A Theology of Metaphor.* Louisville: Westminster John Knox Press, 2002.

deClaissé-Walford, Nancy L. *Reading from the Beginning: The Shaping of the Hebrew Psalter.* Macon GA: Mercer University Press, 1997.

Holladay, William L. *The Psalms through Three Thousand Years: Prayerbook of a Cloud of Witnesses*. Minneapolis: Fortress, 1993.

McCann, J. Clinton. *A Theological Introduction to the Book of Psalms*. Nashville: Abingdon, 1993.

Wisdom Literature

Crenshaw, James. *Old Testament Wisdom: An Introduction*. Louisville: Westminster John Knox Press, 1998.

Gutiérrez, Gustavo. *On Job: God-Talk and the Suffering of the Innocent*. Maryknoll NY: Orbis Books, 1985.

Tamez, Elsa. *When the Horizons Close: Rereading Ecclesiastes*. Maryknoll NY: Orbis Books, 2000.

Prophetic Literature

Berrigan, Daniel. *Jeremiah: The World, the Wound of God*. Minneapolis: Fortress Press, 1999.

Brueggemann, Walter. *Hopeful Imagination: Prophetic Voices in Exile*. Philadelphia: Fortress Press, 1986.

Petersen, David L. *The Prophetic Literature: An Introduction*. Louisville: Westminster John Knox Press, 2002.

Popular Music, the Bible, and Religion

Fillingim, David. *Redneck Liberation: Country Music as Theology*. Macon GA: Mercer University Press, 2003.

Gilmour, Michael J., ed. *Call Me the Seeker: Listening to Religion in Popular Music*. New York: Continuum, 2005.

———. *Tangled Up in the Bible: Bob Dylan and Scripture*. New York: Continuum, 2004.

Roncace, Mark, and Patrick Gray, eds. *Teaching the Bible: Practical Strategies for Classroom Discussion*. Atlanta: Society of Biblical Literature, 2005.

Printed in the USA
CPSIA information can be obtained
at www.ICGtesting.com
LVHW011756131223
766324LV00003B/64